*Edna
Wants you to
have this!,
Cynthia*

Get Organized.
Get Focused.
Get Moving.

How to avoid
productivity potholes

CYNTHIA KYRIAZIS

Although the author and publisher have made every effort to ensure that the information in this book was correct at press time, the author and publisher do not assume and hereby disclaim any liability to any party for any loss, damage, or disruption caused by errors or omissions, whether such errors or omissions result from negligence, accident, or any other cause.

Copyright © 2015 by Cynthia Kyriazis

All rights reserved. No part of this book may be used or reproduced in any manner whatsoever without the prior written permission of the publisher, except in the case of brief quotations embodied in critical articles and reviews.

For more information, to inquire about rights to this or other works, or to purchase copies for special educational, business, or sales promotional uses please write to:

Incorgnito Publishing Press
A division of Market Management Group, LLC
33 S. Wilson Avenue, Suite 113
Pasadena, California 91106

FIRST EDITION

Printed in the United States of America

ISBN: 978-1-944589-04-2

10 9 8 7 6 5 4 3 2 1

DEDICATION

*For my family, who kept me going
when I didn't think I could*

ACKNOWLEDGMENTS

No one succeeds in life or business alone, and I'm certainly no exception. So here goes ...

With much thanks to ...

To Janice and Michael for the opportunity to write this book and get it off my to-do list.

To Dean for volunteering to be my "agent" at such a reasonable fee.

To Rochelle, Deb, Joan, Edna, and Mary Kay for the many glasses of wine and being my BFFs in life and in work.

To Mike, Laura, Carley, Brenna, Zak, Daka, and Sal ... who taught me all about living.

To Emily and everyone at Indigo Wild for the soap, the songs, the smiles, and for keeping me young ... or at least trying to.

To Shawn Kent Hayashi for your friendship and inspiration.

To the entire Wisdo family for everything, all the time.

To all my clients for teaching me so much.

And to the people who never hired me, for teaching me even more about how to be better.

CONTENTS

PREFACE

This is my second book. As soon as I finished my first book, *The Organized Communicator*, I began writing this one because something inside me said I wanted to share more information about getting organized and focused with your time management. Because that's what I love.

I can hear you now.

"Organizing? Time management? Productivity?

She really has a *passion* for this kind of stuff?"

Well ... it's not really about any of that. For me, it's really about helping someone get clear on next steps for improving their personal productivity so they can save their **future** time for more fun things. It's about recapturing time because none of us are getting any more than twenty-four hours on any given day. So for me it's about recapturing time to do what you want to do and not always just what you need to do. It's the fun in life. Yes, that's right. Fun.

For example, getting organized for the sake of getting organized doesn't accomplish much. But if you become more organized at work with your paper, time, space and computer files it creates the skeleton that helps support getting to your goals and priorities quicker. You'll end up having all kinds of future time to do what you want which includes having ... fun.

Before I started my own business I worked for a large corporation. I would repeatedly hear someone saying, "But you're *so* organized," and I would simply respond, "I may be organized, but I'm really just lazy. I hate doing things over and over again because it just wastes my time. I'd rather finish work and be out golfing (or some other fun thing)." You see, getting myself organized was always just a means to an end.

More time for fun.

That was many years ago and the world has changed. Now I have my own business and live in a 24/7 world. But my basic statement still holds true: I'd rather spend the time getting organized and improving my time management habits *now* so that I don't have to work future nights, weekends, and holidays. Whether you're a one-person shop, a small business owner, or an employee of a large company, if you get down to it I suspect my sentiment isn't too different from yours.

Of course the truth is that it's more than just about getting organized for more fun time. Maintaining an organized system is large part of helping you *effectively manage the time* you have available. And it impacts you regardless of your role or the size of company you're in because time management is a core competency. Mastering organizing, time management skills, and developing habits improves your productivity which is a vital business strategy influencing job performance, revenue growth, and gaining a competitive edge.

So with all these thoughts rumbling around in my head, I knew I had to write a second book.

I wrote *Get Organized. Get Focused. Get Moving.* by examining and drawing from three key areas:

1) All the lessons I've learned over the years in working with executives, small business owners and solopreneurs

2) Conversations shared within my professional arena

3) Readings and my own thoughts and observations

My goal in sharing this information is to help you find a way to become and maintain a more productive life. It takes an open mind, willingness to do or try something different, and the courage to make it happen. My hope is that you will experience less stress, frustration and anxiety, and more sales and more ... fun.

Because after all, I have a passion about this stuff, you know.

The Last Word

"Real difficulties can be overcome;
it is only the imaginary ones
that are unconquerable."

Theodore Vail, Industrialist

SECTION 1:
INTRODUCTION

Ready.

Set.

Get Organized.

"It's here somewhere ..."

"I can find anything on this desk ... just give me a minute."

"I've run out of time. Again."

Sound familiar?

Not surprising.

As a Productivity Strategist and Professional Organizing Consultant these are the types of statements I hear all the time from new clients, potential clients, wanna-get-organized-now-but-don't-have-time people ... even family and friends. But that's all okay. Because I understand.

Not only because it's my job to understand, but also because even I say some of these things to myself sometimes. Not often, mind you— but sometimes. Yes, even pros at times get unorganized and end up experiencing the same stresses and frustrations as everyone else. The difference is we know all about ...

- The value of getting organized

- How to set up a system that works

- How to recuperate faster after chaos has visited

- And to our benefit and our clients, how to maintain an organized environment

So how do you become organized if you're challenged?

First and foremost, remember that getting organized is a learned skill. Although it's true that a role model can play an important part in teaching us this skill at a young age, role models don't necessarily lead us down the path of a clutter-free environment.

Secondly, it's about developing strategies and techniques that work for *you*. It's not necessarily a one-size-fits-all approach.

This book will provide information, strategies, and techniques I've used with my clients over the years. But I also want to provide this information using a simple approach. After years of conducting organizing and time management workshops, I've found individuals learn *and remember* lessons when they have one thing to remember and are presented with no more than three things they can do to practice what they just learned.

The last page of each chapter has information to help you simplify some of the concepts you read in the chapter:

The One Thing to Remember:

A productivity principle to live by.

Three Things You Can Do:

To help you take that sometimes difficult first step.

What Are You Going to Do?

Write down your most immediate thought on one thing you can do differently. Research shows if you write it down, you're more likely to remember it and do it!

The Last Word

*"The secret of your future
is hidden in your daily routines."*

Mike Murdock

CHAPTER 1

Disorganization costs you dearly

It was a warm summer afternoon and I was in my office catching up on some things when the phone rang. A woman asked for me by name, but I didn't recognize the voice. She said she had just read an article I had written in a local magazine and needed help. She was desperate. In my business, that could mean anything.

It turned out she and her husband owned a small landscaping company and things were really a "mess." She couldn't get her husband to understand the importance of setting up systems and it was causing all kinds of problems. So we made an appointment for the following week.

When I walked into her office, I saw something like the photo on the next page.

This wasn't her husband's desk. It was hers.

I quickly found out that one of the reasons she called was because they had an employee who had embezzled a fair amount of money.

What I found interesting is she thought it was because they didn't have systems in place, but she didn't include her own workspace in the equation.

As I was standing in her office I looked down and on the corner of her

desk I saw a check. An uncashed check. I kept wondering how many more of those were hidden under the papers on her desktop.

I believe if an employee wants to hurt their employer they can find many ways to do just that—some easier than others. In this case I believed the employee saw the condition of the desk and figured she'd never miss the money until long after the employee was gone.

This is one example of how clutter—at many levels—cost a business owner plenty. It wasn't just the stress of lost money, but also the stress it put on these two people as owners and as a married couple.

Then again, clutter always costs much more than it's worth. It costs ...

- *Money* – The landscape company is one of many. Hard dollars were lost because of organizational clutter. Hard lesson to learn.

- *Time* – We only have twenty-four hours in a day and none of us get one second more or less. If you're constantly re-visiting your cluttered environment, you're wasting time you can't get back—time you could be doing more important (or fun) things.

- *Energy* – Another finite resource. You can stay up late or work weekends to get your work done. But if you do that as a normal course of events, the question becomes one of the quality of your work. Was this your best work? Or was your brain drained from dealing with the unimportant?

- *Lack of Focus* – The one thing you need to work on is the most important thing you need to be doing.

- *Anxiety* – Mostly yours. Not being able to find something you need when you need it produces more anxiety than it's worth.

- *Frustration* – This affects you, but it also affects your colleagues and teammates. One of the biggest grievances I hear is from employees complaining about the delay of getting the promised information in their hands, on time, from a colleague.

- *Image Issues* – Clutter plays a role in how others see you ... whether or not the opinion is justified. It's especially stressful and frustrating to your boss who sees your gone-awry desktop and wonders what you might be missing.

- *Peace of Mind* – This is the bottom line. Seeing the clutter day in and day out can be a reminder of things you haven't done and causes your mind to focus on that rather than what's important.

So get ready. Get set. And let's go.

The One Thing to Remember:

Clutter is symptomatic of *delayed decision making*.

Three Things You Can Do:

1. Be prepared to make decisions.

2. Be prepared to make decisions.

3. Be prepared to make decisions.

Write down *one* thing you're going to do differently or change.

The Last Word

"Nobody procrastinates their way into getting organized."

Unknown

CHAPTER 2

It's like a card game—step by step

This portion of the book is all about organizing yourself and your office.

So what does it mean to **oˈr-ge-nīz**? It means three things:

1. Set up an administrative structure.

2. Arrange by systematic planning and united effort.

3. Form into a complete and functioning whole.

Note that this definition doesn't include anything about having a perfect desk or pristine office environment. It's about developing a structure, process, and system that work to support you in your day-to-day work regardless of workload.

Before I became a professional organizer, I was a regional director of operations for a large corporation. I supervised an administrative staff, one technical manager and his staff, and anywhere from four to nine account managers. Each account manager was working from their home long before it was as common as it is today. They were without administrative support, totally autonomous, and needed to be organized and very self-directed in order to be successful.

Part of the reason I became a professional organizer and productivity coach is because I became interested in why two people of seemingly similar backgrounds and education would evolve into two types of managers—one successful in doing what the job required and one not. I came to realize it had to do with how effectively they managed their information, time, and space.

Frank was a perfect example of someone who organized himself by organizing his information and his office. He knew reaching his goals and objectives were tied to his actions which, in turn, were directly tied to how organized he was, physically and mentally. He was a successful manager and grew within the company for years.

Then there was Steve. Same background as Frank, but never quite able to develop and maintain a system that could lead him to the same results Frank was getting.

Keep in mind that at that time, the technology available to us today had just begun arriving on the scene. However, in today's world most of us are feeling we never have enough time which was the very thing technology was supposed to fix. We seem to be faced with *more* paper, *more* files, *more* chaotic hard drives, and less office space.

Welcome to the "new economy."

But this economy isn't really new. To quote Dr. Thomas Jones, an economic futurist, this technology-driven new economy simply has us doing "more things and different things." In the quest to do "more things and different things" we sometimes produce and print more paper than necessary, use our time ineffectively, clutter our space in the process, and then carry all these habits right into our computer—where we are learning to do "more things and different things."

One thing we do differently is process incoming information—both physical and electronic. What do we do with all this incoming information? The overall strategy used to involve teaching clients to handle today's (snail) mail today. Linda Anderson, President of "Getting Clear," taught me this early in my career. If you don't make decisions about today's mail then tomorrow you have two days' worth of mail, the next day you have three days, and so on. Most of us can visualize this because it's an all too realistic view of our desk in today's workplace. The problem is we don't always get to today's mail today.

So consider this: Your approach toward becoming more organized is something similar to playing cards.

- First, create one pile of cards—a deck.

- Second, shuffle and deal the deck …twice

- Third, sort and organize the cards in your hand based on the game you're playing.

- Fourth, decide or prioritize the card to play.

- Fifth, play the card giving you the best advantage for winning.

If you organize yourself—keeping this card game approach in mind—you consciously begin managing all that information that's coming at you. If you do it out of order—say, sort the cards and then for some reason shuffle—clutter begins showing up. You lose the game.

This book is about learning these steps to win your game.

Your Deck

So let's go back to the landscaping company.

The very first thing I did was put all her cards in one pile. All that paper that was scattered across her desk was *not* one project.

As Odette Pollar said in her book, *Time Management Systems*,

> *"Clutter is not one project all spread out.*
> *Clutter is unrelated stuff mixed together."*

More often than not what I find with a client is information requiring *action* or *filing* and information needing to be *discarded* or *deleted* are all stored together on the top of the desk or an e-mail inbox. Result? Cluttered desktop. Cluttered hard drive. Cluttered mind.

Co-mingling and re-visiting information over and over again looking for something specific is an enormous waste of time. And that time lost doesn't happen in one big chunk. It happens as you keep returning to the information over and over, several times an hour, spending a couple minutes here and a couple minutes there, day in and day out. Dribs and drabs, as I call it.

So back to the card game. When you're ready to play cards you need one deck. Same approach with information coming into your office.

What to do?

Electronically, it's easy because all your e-mail automatically ends up in one inbox.

Voice-mail is easy too for the same reason.

Paper? Not as easy. Incoming paper tends to land in several places. Sometimes it's the corner of your desk, sometimes it's your chair, sometimes it's the floor and sometimes it's your window ledge. You get the idea. Without a system, it lands everywhere.

Identify one location to store incoming information and then store it there. Every time. All the time. This sounds really simple, doesn't it? Not for some. Yet it's a critical first step. Remember you need a deck of cards to begin playing—not cards lying all around the table.

The One Thing to Remember:

Consistently store all incoming information in one location.

20

Three Things You Can Do:

1. Create a home for incoming paper using a tray, basket, box ... whatever works for you.

2. Begin creating a habit of storing incoming paper in that location.

3. Always, always, always move information forward to the next required action, not back into where it came from. More on that in the next chapter.

Write down *one* thing you're going to do differently or change.

The Last Word

*"The secret of getting ahead is getting started.
The secret of getting started is breaking your complex
overwhelming tasks into small, manageable tasks
and then starting on the first one."*

Mark Twain, Author and Humorist

CHAPTER 3

Stop shuffling and start dealing

So you've begun putting your incoming paper in one spot, just like having all the cards in one deck. Now it's time to shuffle your cards/papers.

You have pile of paper and each piece of paper requires a decision in order to move it forward to its next logical location. And by "move it forward" I'm not talking about looking through your pile and picking out one or two pieces of paper that can be easily handled. I'm not talking about selectively dealing with some e-mail or voice-mail and not others—no matter how tempting that may be. *Looking at information and putting it back where it came from and doing so multiple times a day just wastes time. Your* time.

Stop Shuffling

You already know that maintaining a cluttered environment costs money, time, and energy, and it causes lack of focus, anxiety, frustration, image, and peace of mind. Yet it remains one of the most problematic issues when it comes to personal job performance.

My client Dean was really good at piling his incoming information but it seemed each time I came to his office the pile hadn't gone down. Sometimes it went up. So I watched him work at his desk one day and discovered why.

Dean would pick up a paper, read it, put it back down where he got it from and then go to another piece of paper and do exactly the same thing. This was a serious time waster and I was sure he didn't realize what it was costing him in time, focus, and energy. He hadn't stopped to think about the how many minutes an hour, day in and day out, he spent going through this routine. Dribs and drabs.

So I pointed it out to him, we talked about it, and he got much better at making decisions for moving his paper to the next step.

But there was another surprise waiting for me.

At the next visit I realized that what he was doing with paper he was also doing with e-mail. Reading it and coming back to it later to re-read it. Then going to the next e-mail and doing the same. Again and again. He kept shuffling his information. The e-mail inbox was looking suspiciously similar to the paper inbox. Visiting and revisiting e-mail costs precious time and energy—time and energy Dean could have used for working on what's important.

Over the course of time, I've witnessed this scenario again and again. And it's not only the consistent re-visiting of e-mails but another issue as well. I see the e-mail inbox used as a to-do list, a research mechanism, an address book, a calendar, etc. You name it. A catch-all.

Remember: paper, time, space, and technology are all intercon-nected. If managing your paper challenges you, you may also be challenged by managing your electronic files. The same habits seem to carry forth.

Although it's not true all the time, I frequently see clutter on top of the desk and corresponding clutter in the hard drive. Conversely, if you're effective at managing yourself with the time you have, you probably do well with managing your paper and space.

It's important to understand this concept because if you believe your systems are exclusive you create an imbalance which can and usually does lead to roadblocks. So here's the second step in getting organized—stop shuffling and learn to *deal the cards* in your deck so you can eliminate that pile of paper facing you.

Dealing the Cards

You're going to deal your paper out twice.

First deal. You deal your pile by making only one of four decisions for each piece of paper you touch. I call it the **AFTR** approach. Because after you're done with these decisions you'll begin creating a system for yourself.

Here are your four choices:

> Act
> File
> Trash
> Read

- *Act* – This is something that requires YOUR action in the form of a response, research, etc.

- *File* – Filing has a much lower priority than other things you do during the day and week, so for this reason I suggest a pile. Of course, how *high* the pile should get is covered in the chapter on filing. For now, you can create a file pile.

- *Trash* – Self-explanatory. Grab the information you need from the document and put it in your calendar or CRM and get rid of the paper or e-mail that brought it to you.

- *Read* – Reading is important but also tends to have a lower priority. Keeping it in a pile makes it easy to grab when you identify time for reading. Again, how *high* the pile gets will be covered in the chapter on filing.

Once you deal your pile, you'll see only one pile remaining and it will be your Act pile. Things that *you* need to do.

Second deal. Now take your Act pile and deal again by asking yourself what the VERY next logical thing that has to happen with that paper. This is about sorting your actions to help you further refine your system. Some suggestions for action piles include phone calls, computer work, research, errands, personal, etc.

Here's an example:

I was driving to an event to speak and my car broke down. There were lots of things that ran across my mind. I needed to call the event organizer, AAA for a tow, my mechanic, and my family. But of all those things to do, the *very* next thing I had to do was call AAA so I could get safely off the road.

Calling the event organizer, my mechanic, and my family were all very important but the *very* next thing I needed to do was look out for my safety.

Same is true with your Act pile. This pile represents all the things you need to do which can include phone calls, e-mails, research, delegating to others, notes from meetings, travel plans, etc. Dealing and sorting begins creating what I like to call your administrative skeleton. And this is done by grouping similar things/actions together.

Let me repeat that.
You need to deal and sort this information by grouping similar things/actions together.

For example, you sort all your phone calls together, meeting notes together, things to give to your teammates, things to discuss with your boss, errands to run, etc. It's whatever your work life requires.

Why?

Because *grouping similar things/actions together is the basis of all time management programs.*

It's a main strategy in managing information overload and a key element in learning to become an effective manager of yourself and your time.

Think about it. Your calendar sorts your days. Your appointments sort your time. You sort clean clothes from the dirty clothes. You sort nails by size. Similar things grouped together create systems you need to begin creating a process or daily routine.

At this point in my presentations attendees are polite, but may have a quizzical look on their face. And you may be doing the same thing. So let me take you on a tour of your kitchen.

If I blindfolded you and stood you in the middle of your kitchen and asked you to make dinner and set the table, chances are you could probably do it.

Why?

Because you generally have a system in your kitchen where items are sorted with similar things are grouped together. For example: pots and pans in one place, canned goods in another, silverware in one spot, dishes in another, and glasses in yet another. All grouped together by item and stored in their home base.

So you go begin the creative process of making a meal, setting the table, and eating. When you're done, you wash the plates and cups or put them in the dishwasher. When they're clean and dried, you put them back in their stored location or home base.

Why?

So when you come home tomorrow, you can make another meal without wasting a lot of time. Without recreating the proverbial wheel. There's a system. There's a process.

This exact scenario is what happens on your desktop every single day.

You "cook" or create scenarios on your desktop all day long. You have incoming information hitting you at every turn, projects with deadlines, priorities that keep shifting, and potential emergencies all taking up pieces of your very limited time.

Sorting and storing things to create a system and process is what begins creating an administrative structure you can use day in and day out. Automatically. Without using a lot of your precious brain power.

Building this system for yourself ...

o Creates a home base for information so you can retrieve it more easily

o Eliminates a lot of clutter

o Provides visual groupings and a shorthand for what actions you need to take next

o Enables you to begin creating a workable, user-friendly system to support you regardless of your workload.

So stop shuffling all that paper, deal the deck twice, and get ready to move to the next step.

The One Thing to Remember:

Sorting is the basis of *all* time management programs.

Three Things You Can Do:

1. Deal or sort by grouping similar things together.

2. First deal – use the AFTR technique.

3. Second deal—be prepared to make a decision about the *very* next action you need to take.

Write down *one* thing you're going to do differently or change.

The Last Word

"A system permits ordinary people to achieve extraordinary results."

Bob Burg

CHAPTER 4

Where do you store information?

I've already shared with you that paper, time, and space are all interconnected. A challenge in one area can result in a challenge in another. Now that you have paper sorted where do you put it?

When you want to go someplace, you use a road map. And that's exactly what I use when working with a client. There are two types. First, an Office Road Map which is about where to place your office furniture to create a user friendly and productive environment. And second, an Information Road Map which is about where paper is stored.

Office Road Map

The average size of an office keeps getting smaller and is now down to around 156 square feet. Not much room. Part of the reason for this is we store more information electronically. Somehow I haven't seen this translate into less paper on the desktop or in the office. If anything, it appears there's more. So space needs to be used wisely.

Most effective furniture layout: A U-shaped desk configuration is the most effective.

This is an example of a U-shaped configuration (with the "U" on its side in this picture).

A U-shaped furniture arrangement enables your chair to become "mission control" so by turning your chair you can access just about anything without getting up and interrupting yourself.

The next most effective layout: An L-shaped furniture arrangement.

If you don't have room to arrange your office furniture in this U-shape configuration, the L-shape is the next best thing. This is how most offices existed before computers came into the mix. If you need more surface space and/or file space, you can always add a two-drawer file at one or both ends of your desk.

Ergonomics

We sit at our desks for long hours every day. Making your workspace comfortable is just part of the equation. Another important thing to consider is if your arrangement is preventing you from sustaining permanent injury like carpal tunnel syndrome, lower back problems, and eye strain. It's about ergonomics.

According to Merriam Webster, ergonomics is defined as ...

An applied science concerned with designing and arranging things people use so that the people and things interact most efficiently and safely.

It has to do with how desks, monitors, keyboards, chairs, and lighting affect your body and health.

Unfortunately if ergonomics isn't taken into account when setting up an office, the long-term consequences can eventually require surgery, as in the case of carpal tunnel. Here are some ergonomic guidelines to follow:

Seating
- Chair with a waterfall front edge
- Feet and elbows at 90-degree angles
- Thighs and arms are bent to rest parallel to floor
- Backrest should support the lower lumbar area
- Bottom of elbows should be about the same height as the keyboard

Work Surface Height
- Adjusted base should be 24" to 32"

- Reading, writing, and phone should be at 28" to 29"
- Keyboard and mouse level should be 26" to 27" from the floor

Monitor Placement

- Top of monitor should be at eye level, about 25" away
- Vertical location should be 15–50 degrees below horizontal eye level
- Tilt top of monitor, not your head
- Adjust for glare through the use of glare screens

Lighting

- Ambient or overhead lighting should be kept low
- Task lighting should supplement ambient light
- Natural light reduces glare dependent on placement of monitor and use of glare screens

Another thing that has been well documented is what happens when we sit too long without standing up or taking our eyes off the computer monitor. The key here is breaking up and doing several things during your day that require changing from sitting to standing to stretching because too much sitting OR too much standing can lead to conditions of inflammation and other chronic conditions. The problem is becoming acute so you now have several choices for stand-up desks and sit-stand work products. You might also want to consider walking meetings.

Alan Hedge, a professor of ergonomics at Cornell University, tells us that, so make sure you mix things up. He suggests that for every thirty minutes, sit for twenty minutes, stand for eight minutes, and stretch for two minutes.

Information Road Map

Storing and accessing information (or supplies) is based on *frequency of usage*. Just take a cue from grocery stores. The more popular an item, the more likely it will be placed at eye level. So the more frequently you reach for something in your office, the closer at hand it should be stored.

I call these Levels of Access and there are four of them.

- **Level 1: Current information**

  This is information or supplies you touch on a regular basis or several times a week, so this area is easily and logically accessible to you. In this area you'd store things like pens, pencils, stapler, etc. But it's also where you can store binders of information you grab regularly. These reference binders are a more organized option than cluttered bulletin boards.

- **Level 2: Project information**

  We're pretty much project-driven in today's workplace when it comes to creating a need to store information for easy access to multiple projects. You may work on a project several times in one week or only once in a while, but storing project information in one area is the most effective approach. This area is generally located on top of your desk rather than inside desk drawers. In the past this space was usually a credenza located behind your chair. But in today's offices this space could be behind you or to the side.

- **Level 3: Reference information**

  This type of information is something you may need to refer to from time to time but not necessarily daily. It represents your library of information. It's important and needs to be kept within arms reach in a file cabinet in your office.

- **Level 4: Archive information**

  This level of access represents information that's important—

usually financial, legal, or technical—and needs to be maintained but not accessed very often. This could be a file cabinet outside of your office—down the hall, in a central file system, in a basement—or off premises. Old tax documents or expired contracts would be a good example. Check with your supervisor to understand how this type of information is defined and managed within your organization.

Prime Realty

Every desk has a Prime Realty area—a term I picked up from a friend in real estate who's always talking to me about prime areas.

Your desk has Prime Realty. It's the space where you do your work. It's where you focus when you're not on the computer. And it needs to be kept clutter free because clutter distracts and clutter can cause information to seemingly disappear.

So here's the scenario. You're working on something in your Prime Realty space and someone comes into your office. Priorities shift. You need to stop what you're doing, shift your focus, and start doing something else.

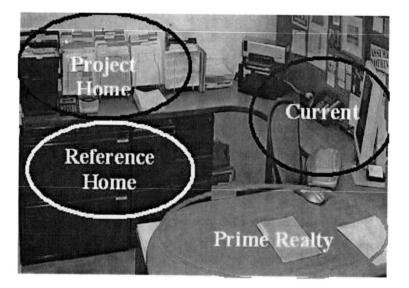

Take those papers you were working on in your Prime Realty area and put them *back in their home*. Wherever you identified that project's storage location. In this case, it might be where you store projects, on the surface of your desk, to the left or right (see image on next page). Putting them on a windowsill, a chair, or the corner of your desk isn't a great idea. And you might forget where you put them and then somehow they disappear. So when asking yourself the inevitable "where did I put those papers?" question, it doesn't become a multiple-choice answer. If you have one consistent location for storing and retrieving papers or files, the answer is easy.

Stop the disappearing paper syndrome today!

The One Thing to Remember:

Storage guidelines are based on frequency of usage.

Three Things You Can Do:

1. Identify your four levels of access.

2. Store things you touch several times a week on the surface.

3. Identify your Prime Realty area.

Write down *one* thing you're going to do differently or change.

The Last Word

*"It's so hard when contemplated in advance
and so easy when you do it."*

Robert M. Pirsig

CHAPTER 5

How you store information depends on your *style*

The last chapter was about *where* you store information. This chapter is about *how* you store information. It's time to arrange the cards in your hand.

Doesn't sound very important, does it?

How you store your information can make a big difference between simply setting up a system and setting up a user-friendly system so you can successfully *maintain* it. So you can play the cards in your hand and win.

In the past few years, profiling candidates and employees through assessments has become an integral part of business. We assess behaviors, psychological makeup, and emotional responsiveness and communication styles just to name a few. Over the years I've found that how you store information is not a one-size-fits-all approach. It seems to be very much based on *style*.

Your Style of Organizing

Did you even know you had a paper management *style?*

Most of us don't. In my field of work I see it on a regular basis.

Observing and analyzing patterns is an important part of what I do. Very early in my career I observed my managers and what they did and didn't do to help themselves be successful ... or not. This skill set has served me well over the years because each client is different.

My client base includes everything from a solopreneurs to NFL players. Yup. So watching what makes them tick is part of the fun.

And the person I learned this from was ... me.

When I left corporate America I also left behind my administrative assistant. Alexandra—Alex for short—was a gift from heaven. Very organized, very on top of things, and kept both me and my schedule in working order. She was amazing.

Then I went to work for myself. No Alex. Just me.

So I set up my office. Bought furniture, files, and containers to hold things. You get the picture.

But it wasn't working.

I wasn't able to find things. Very unusual for me. Trouble is, I couldn't figure out why this was happening. And slowly the dawn of realization began creeping in. The types of things I was doing as an entrepreneur were different than the types of things I was doing as an employee. With or without Alex, my work life was different and so were my organizational and time management challenges.

So I began observing and analyzing *my own* patterns. It seemed the problem for me was how I was storing my information. Seriously.

When this "ah-ha" light came on, I started watching my clients. And it appeared to be exactly the same issue.

It became really clear to me when working with two clients who were job sharing. Their organization took one full-time job and split the hours so each employee worked twenty hours a week. They shared a desk. The odd couple in action. Do you see where this is going?

One person wanted to store her files horizontally in piles. The other wanted to store her files vertically by standing them in a vertical container. It seemed to be the same issue I experienced in my newfound entrepreneurial office. Hmm.

So after seeing this time and again, I developed a ten-question true/false quiz I use during my workshops.

Highly scientific? No.

Does it provide some information about how you prefer to store paper? Yes!

So take a minute to take my P.O.P. quiz to help you learn about your Personal Organizing Profile.

Personal Organizing Profile Quiz

Answer each question TRUE or FALSE and tally your answers up at the bottom. This quiz is based on your preferences so there are *no right or wrong answers*. Your initial response is best.

1. I prefer having my files surrounding me on top of my desk rather than inside file cabinets.

2. I don't mind using manila file folders as long as they are labeled, but I really would rather have colored file folders.

3. I almost can't live without Post-it notes to remind me of things.

4. I prefer keeping my papers and files in baskets or sorting bins.

5. When I put my files in a filing cabinet I tend to forget they are even there.

6. I tend to identify a file by a project or a person associated with the project rather than alphabetically.

7. I generally don't mind handling several projects at once, rather than one at a time.

8. Most of the time, I tend to lose track of time when working on a project.

9. I don't readily throw things out.

10. I just love to-do lists.

TOTAL:

True_____ False _____

© 2016 Productivity Partners Inc.

Now hold on to that information for a minute.

One Style

I received a phone call from John, a purchasing agent for a very large construction company. He was referred to me hoping I could help because he was afraid he was going to lose his job.

He explained that he'd been with his company for many years but had a new boss and John's disorganization was becoming a problem for him. He asked me to come to his office at 5:30 p.m. after everyone had left. He didn't want his boss to know.

When I got there the problem was fairly evident.

I looked in his office and going clockwise this is what I saw:

- A table with all kinds of things on it

- A bookcase with everything except books

- A chair with papers

- A desk with more papers

- A desk filing drawer with tennis shoes in it

- A computer with Post-it notes all the way around the monitor

- A window ledge filled with piles of papers two to three feet high

- A two-drawer lateral file cabinet with all the files *on top* of the cabinet. The inside of the cabinet had empty green hanging folders

- Another chair with more papers

40

- A cleared path on the floor for me to walk into his office

I never took a picture, but you get the idea.

I ask clients not to clean up their desk before I get to their office because I can learn a lot by looking at the natural state. So as I usually do, I started asking questions. Lots of questions. And here's what I found out.

John was a strategic purchasing agent. He dealt with bigger, broader concepts involving more than a single purchase. His job was to figure out how to get the best price and the best product not only for existing projects, but also for future projects. He had to anticipate future needs and was paid to be more of a strategic thinker than an implementation person.

Although he had a good relationship with the owner, he had a new boss named Andrew. And Andrew was not an organizing slouch. If you asked him for information he could produce it in seconds. He knew right where everything was in his office and how to get to it. And he held others to the same level of expectation.

The problem is when Andrew would come to John's office and ask for some piece of information, John couldn't find it. He'd look and look but just couldn't retrieve it. Andrew would get tired of waiting ... and watching ... and tell John when he found the information to bring it to Andrew's office on the third floor.

This had happened several times. Although John's previous performance reviews were great, he started to fear his new boss might not see it that way.

But there was something I observed in John's office that had my curiosity. It looked like he *had* set up a system at some point in time and for some reason the system failed. The system he set up simply wasn't working for him.

Why?

Because John was very visually cued. That's why the paper and files in his office were on the surface and not inside the filing drawers. He simply forgot what and where things were stored.

So he tried to fix this and actually made it worse. He began creating one file folder for *every piece of paper* thinking it would help him more easily retrieve the information he needed. This created hundreds and hundreds of files. He couldn't file. He couldn't retrieve. He had pressure and deadlines. He was overwhelmed.

What now?

I honored John's visual style. This style responds to visual cues rather than folders with label names.

Here are a few of the things we changed:

- **Placement as a Trigger**
  I used on-surface trays, inboxes, and sorters. This helped him store things he could see so he could effectively retrieve them.

- **Color as a Trigger**
  Color doesn't cue some people but it worked for John. Priority items were put in one color file folder; completed files were put in another, etc.

- **Completed Projects**
  We agreed if construction was completed, bills paid, and project closed, the project files would be stored inside the filing cabinet and not anywhere else. Active files remained on the surface in their own type of visual storage containers.

- **Use Technology**
  To create his paper filing system. More on this in my chapter on filing systems.

- **Create A Simple Routine and Checklist**
  To help him maintain the system long after I was gone.

Some people, like John, are visually cued. Others respond to language cues like file folders with labels on them. And yet others seem to use both visual and language cues.

When I first started my business I called this Left Brain, Right Brain, Whole Brain styles of organizing. Today some research suggests that it has nothing to do with the side of the brain; it's just a preference.

If you go back to the quiz you took at the beginning of this chapter, here's how to score it:

- Seven or more true – You tend to need visual cues. I call this the **Piler style** (right-brain tendencies).

- Seven or more false – You tend to need language cues. I call this the **Filer style** (left-brained tendencies).

- Any other combination of answers probably means you're both a Piler and a Filer, or your style uses both visual and language cues. I call this the **Combo style** (whole-brained tendencies—or as one workshop attendee asked, "Does that mean we *have* a brain?").

Pilers

If you're not a Piler, you probably know someone who is. They're usually the person who has multiple piles around their office and can sometimes reach for that exact piece of paper they need in any one of those piles.

This is Carley's office. She worked in a department of twelve people within a large pharmaceutical company. Eleven of the employees in this department were research scientists. She was the only graphic illustrator and found herself struggling to keep from dropping projects, forgetting projects, or making deadlines, not to mention the comments made about the condition of her desk.

Because she's a graphic illustrator she tends to react to visual cues, so we changed how she stored her information by storing items visually using trays and sorting bins of various sizes and kinds.

This sorting also translated into how she was managing her time. She began putting more deadline information in one place ... her calendar. It was a win/win all the way around.

Some Ideas for Pilers

- **Placement**
  Storing information that lies horizontally on your desk is generally better for you. The file on the upper right corner of your desk can mean something different than the one on the upper left corner.

- **Containers**
  Storing information lying down and visible works for you. Trays, boxes, baskets, sorters ... anything that can contain the paper.

  Here's a picture of a literature sorter, and it works well for Pilers:

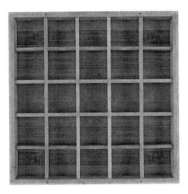

- **Color**
  Just as I used it for John, it might work for you. However, using more than four colors can get really confusing ... even for you.

- **Computer Storage**
  This way Pilers know where they *store* their information. Unless their hard drive is organized, they may not always *find* their information. This method works especially well with those who have Attention Deficit Disorder (ADD) and strong search mechanisms.

- **Create a Routine for Maintenance**
  Put a recurring event on your calendar to remind yourself to clean out! This helps prevent piles that are so high they fall over. Things may move from surface to file cabinet to trash. Just remember to be consistent with these reviews.

Filers

If visual retrieval isn't your style then you may prefer labels on file folders. Someone usually asks me if that means this style is more organized.

Not really.

Consider my client Michael. He owned a real estate development company that was new and growing fast but needed help with filing mostly his financial papers. I realized for him filing wasn't a priority and wasn't nearly as much fun as growing his business but he knew it needed to get done. I also realized he was cued by labels, not piles. Each time I came to his office his desk was cleaned off and what was there was what he was working on at the moment.

Then one day I dropped by unexpectedly and his desk looked something like this:

His secret to having me think he was organized? When he knew I was coming he'd open the drawers and cabinets and hide his paperwork.

When he admitted that, we both had a good laugh.

Michael was a very linear thinker who responded to file folders with labels when it came to his financials, but that didn't mean he was organized!

Some Ideas for Filers:

- **Placement**
  This can be used easily, but sparingly. Too many folders on the desktop tend to disrupt your style of thinking!

- **Containers**
  Storing in formation standing up works better for you. Avoid trays, boxes, baskets, and go for anything that holds files vertically so you can see the label.

- **Color**
  This doesn't really cue Filers unless it's just one or two files.

- **Computer**
  Storing information here works well because you use file names to retrieve. Your style generally arranges their electronic files with a sense of organization.

- **Creating a Routine for Maintenance**
  Filers are pretty good about maintaining their space because clutter disrupts their thinking. However, put a recurring event on your calendar to remind yourself that it's time to clean out

reading piles, filing piles, and filing cabinets so you can become consistent rather than trying to do this all in one day.

Combos

And finally, if you're someone who is cued by both visuals and language you may have the toughest job of all. You need to figure out what things to store on the surface in piles and what things to store vertically or in binders and file cabinets.

Remember my story when I started my business and couldn't find things in my own office?

Well, I realized from taking my own quiz that I'm a Combo. Here's what I discovered.

Work In Progress

I needed this information to be stored on the surface of my desk lying down. This included things like writing a book, creating a new training, waiting for a return call, etc.

- **Completed or Things I Needed to Reference**
  I needed these files stored in file cabinets in my office. This included things like a list of passwords, prior client files, etc. The reason for this approach for myself is partially because too much paper on my desk tends to distract me. But the more important part of this is that I considered completed projects to be stored separately and not in eye's view.

- **Historical**
  I stored these in file cabinets in a completely separate area of the office and not in my immediate workspace. These included old financials, incorporation papers, technical information, etc.

Some Ideas for Combos:

- **Placement**
  Use one side of your desk for one thing and the other for another. I use the left side of my desk for "waiting to hear from someone" and the right side for "works in progress."

- **Containers**
  Files stored vertically and horizontally both work for you. Your job is to determine which ones go which way!

  Here's a picture of a rolling file cabinet. I've always maintained at least a couple of these in my office because it works for both visual and language styles ... and it rolls so it can move around your office if needed.

  Try to buy the ones made of steel. They're more of an investment, but the plastic ones end to fall apart very quickly from the weight of the paper.

- **Color**
  Sometimes it works for you and sometimes it doesn't. Here are a couple of products that take both language and color into consideration:

- **Computer**
  Filers generally like electronic filing systems. And they tend to organize them.

- **Creating a Routine for Maintenance**
  Combos are pretty good about maintaining their workspace. However, they still need to put it on their calendar for a regular and ongoing review.

So now you know about where to store your information as well as how to store it according to your style. These are two important pieces of information to help you not only store and find things, but also to keep clutter away.

Style Challenges

In organizations that have job sharing, from time to time I'm asked how to deal with two employees who share a desk but have different styles. This can be tricky, but it comes down to communicating a couple agreed upon rules. I usually suggest the two employees sit down and answer the following questions based on what I've outlined in this chapter:

- Are you a Piler, Filer, or Combo?

- Where do you generally store priority documents?

Once this is understood and discussed, agree on what the desktop will look like at the end of each shift. Create simple, clear guidelines setting expectations that when each employee leaves for the day, everything is stored on the desktop in the agreed upon manner. This way expectations are set ahead of time about what happens at the end of the day so the person coming in has no surprises or has to waste time looking for things.

If employees are sharing office space, they are also probably sharing physical and electronic files. So how do they store them to be able to find them?

o   If the employees share a *physical* filing cabinet, I recommend The Paper Tiger filing software system because each person can add their *own* keywords to find things. Style won't matter.

o   If the employees share an *electronic* filing system, it takes a bit more work, but The Paper Tiger will work here as well. If not, the employees can rely on search or they can sit down and agree on category and sub-category names.

Another question I get asked from time to time is how to handle an employee on a team who is unorganized. I think an effective question to ask is how is this person's disorganization causing a problem for the team? If it's that the person misses deadlines, doesn't come to meetings on time, and doesn't produce the work they were responsible for then these are situations where their disorganization is affecting the team.

Like any other discussion around job performance, it's good to begin by asking why they're having difficulty and taking the time to fully understand their challenges and issues. Once this is understood, the employee can be given help in the form of education, mentors, or coaches to help them overcome the key issues.

However, if the employee's actions don't impact any of the items above, then it's a matter of learning to perhaps overlook their approach. I had a case like this years ago and still remember it.

I was called in to work with a woman whose boss was very concerned about her messy desk. She had a normal size cubicle, down the hall from her boss, so every time he walked by he saw her office.

When I got there I began asking my normal questions to see if this was negatively impacting either her performance or the productivity of her teammates or department. Each time the answer was no. Her take on it was that she had a supervisor who liked to maintain a clutter-free, almost paper free, desktop and office. So each time they walked past the employee's office, the "clutter" on the employee's desk sent up a flag of concern that the employee might be "missing" something. Or she wouldn't make a deadline, etc. However, none of that was true when I questioned the supervisor later.

In this case, I suggested that at the end of the day the employee gather all the papers on top of her desk and store them all in a tray or accordion file for the evening. This way her desk would be clear when she walked in her office in the morning and it would help the supervisor feel better and less stressed about how it looked as he walked in and out of the office.

As always, situations like this should be taken on a case-by-case basis.

The One Thing to Remember:

Identify your style of paper management and honor it.

Three Things You Can Do:

1. If your current desktop setup supports you in being organized and productive, leave it alone. No need to change it.

2. If your current desktop setup doesn't work to support you, customize it according to your style.

3. Understand different styles and be tolerant of them because it's not a one-size-fits-all approach.

Write down *one* thing you're going to do differently or change.

The Last Word

"Organizing is what you do when you do something
so when you do it it's not all mixed up."

Winnie the Pooh

CHAPTER 6

Organizing a *paper* filing system, because yes ... we still have paper

The average corporation has about nineteen copies of a given document. A full four-drawer filing cabinet contains 18,000 pieces of paper.

The Gartner Group says it costs about $25,000 to fill a four-drawer filing cabinet and over $2,100 a year to maintain it. Remember, your costs include the cost of the filing cabinet, the cost of the square footage when you keep adding filing cabinets, and the time invested by yourself and others looking for information and replicating documents you can't find.

Using our definition of **or-ge-nīzed**, filing systems help you arrange your system in a "united effort" and "form a complete and functioning whole." So with this in mind, I wouldn't call this an effective filing system:

This employee worked for a Fortune 500 company and failed to make enough decisions about what to do with their files so their storage ended up overflowing from the filing cabinets to the floor.

Here's another filing system. Not.

This was the filing cabinet of small businessman who entered a Messy Desk contest run by a TV station years ago. If you look closely, you can see the box labeled "1999." This was his office manager's attempt at putting all the financials in one place, as she explained it, "In case we get called by the IRS for an audit!"

I was hired as the consultant to help this person get his office organized. I had people helping me the day of the contest and in four hours we were able to help make his office and "filing cabinet" *look* organized. Remember, it was television.

By the way, here's a picture of the owner's office:

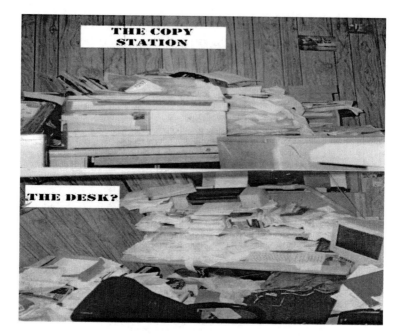

But what about his electronic files? The owner of a full electronic filing cabinet frequently has the same issues as someone with a full paper filing cabinet. Namely, clutter.

Although the cost of technology is less, the time spent filing, retrieving, and maintaining electronic files can rival any paper system. In time and in money.

But as I say, it isn't really about filing something. It's about *finding* something. When you need it. Every time.

Filing Systems

Let's begin by identifying the four types of filing systems available to you and how they're used:

○ **Archival System**

Holds information from the *past*. These files aren't accessed very frequently and can be found stored in either a central filing system on premises, an offsite warehouse, or off premises through companies like Iron Mountain, which store your documents for a fee.

○ **Tickler System**

Holds information for the *future*. I've been asked many times how this filing system got its name and I haven't been able to find out. I'm guessing it's because it comes back to remind you of something you need in the future.

What I do know is that the most successful people I've ever known maintained this type of system. But warning: Pilers don't necessarily love this system because there is more than one step involved. They prefer one and done.

You can buy a folder or sorter to use as a Tickler file from a big box store that looks like this:

You can also set up your system with just a few file folders. Here's how:

1. **Label thirty-one file folders 1 through 31.** This represents the number of days in a month.

2. **Label twelve additional file folders.** These have the name of the month—January, February, etc.

3. **Put the thirty-one file folders in a filing drawer or rolling cart.** Store the twelve file folders behind it. I use a rolling cart because I'm frequently in and out of this folder daily.

4. **For documents you want or need again during the *current* month, file it in the file folder with that specific date.** So if the current month was March and you needed it for the 7th, you would store it in the file marked 7. Frequently I'll put that date in the upper right corner of the document and circle it.

5. **For documents you need in the future, i.e., paper files, tickets, bills, and birthday cards, store it in the appropriate *monthly* file folder.**

6. **On the first of every month, move information from the *monthly* folder to the current *daily* folder (1-31 folder).** Yes, you may need to look at your calendar to make sure the dates are still good, but that's easy.

Using Your Tickler System

I check my Tickler every morning and grab what I need for the day. I check it again before I leave my office and pull out whatever I want sitting on my desk for the next morning. If you're traveling it's important to put the documents you need for your travel in your system for the last day you'll be in the office before traveling. You could even put all those documents in a certain color of file folder so you know when you see it that it's for travel. In reality, if you're using a Tickler system effectively, you'll probably be in and out of it during most days because dates and requirements change. That's why I use a rolling cart for my Tickler system. It stops me from having to open and close a file drawer several times a day.

Setting up a Tickler system is easy, but I've found that using and maintaining one doesn't work for everyone. Training yourself to use it can be a challenge, but I believe it's well worth the investment. You don't have to "remember" to take files—the Tickler file remembers for you.

The Tickler system saves your brain. Something like "set it and forget it." You put the information in a system and forget about it again until you need it. You don't have to worry about where you stored it for the future. That's why I think very successful people like the system. Their brains aren't taxed with minutiae.

o **Functional System**

Holds information that is *current*. Files can be organized several different ways depending on industry, profession, and personal preference. For example, the most popular is an alpha system, but you could also arrange numerically, alpha-numerically, chronologically, or geographically. This type of system usually has major categories as well as sub-categories.

But there's a secret to maintaining these files.

What is it?

Maintaining an effective system requires you to limit the number of broad-based categories to no more than seven. You can have as many sub-categories as you want or need, but limiting the initial decision to seven or less makes it much easier for the brain to make a preliminary decision and then "hunt." And research has proved there is some truth to this. If you follow this simple trick, you develop a much more effective and user-friendly system. I have clients who contact me years later to tell me they still use this approach and it's still working for them.

By broad-based category names, I mean categories such as HR, Administrative, Sales, Financial, Personal, etc. As an example, sub-categories to HR could include Comp and Benefits, Recruiting, Hiring, etc. Also, for some industries and organizations, HR might be a sub-category to Administrative; Sales might be a sub-category to Financial, and so on.

And as I remind everyone in my workshops ...

"Miscellaneous" and **"Other"** are NOT category names!

o   **Digital System**

Holds *electronic* information. Your company may already have guidelines for naming and archiving digital files so be sure to check with your supervisor. More on digital filing systems in the next chapter.

If you still have concerns and doubts about taking the time to set up a paper filing system, here's my secret to the most user-friendly, effective, time-saving, and productive filing system I know. In fact, it's the only system I use for myself and for clients who are willing to take the time to understand and appreciate its power.

The Paper Tiger

The most effective way to work with filing system is to *create and maintain an index* of what is in the filing cabinet. Very large and sophisticated company-wide filing systems have this built into their specialized software. The Paper Tiger software is a filing system in a box and helps you create an index for your files ... even if you're a one-person shop. It's easy, it's reasonably priced, and it works.

Paper Tiger is based on a numerical hanging file system. Each hanging file has a number inserted on a plastic tab affixed to the hanging file—1, 2, 3, 4, etc. The index provided through the software is a mirror reflection of what you have in your hanging files. So whatever is stored in hanging file #1 is also listed in the index.

I can hear you now. If it's numerical, how do I know what's in the file drawer when I open it?

That's the power of technology and The Paper Tiger.

The application has a keyword search feature. So you type in the word of the file you're looking for—the word you put into the index—and in *five seconds or less* it tells you in which hanging file you can find your information. You can put up to 2,000 keywords in the index. So if you call it the *Ford* and another employee calls it the *truck* and another calls it a *van,* all those keywords can be added to the index and anyone can find what they're looking for.

You can:

- Create the index alphabetically or numerically

- Create multiple filing systems

- Create finding system for any collectible—CDs, books, recipes—anything that can have a number adhered to it

- Limit who inputs information

- Limit who revises information

There are many different ways to set up Paper Tiger to get it to work for you.

The point is that it is a *finding* system for you at the tip of your fingers. It's user friendly, customizable, and saves time and money.

My kind of product.

But how long does it take to set it up?

This depends on how many files you have and whether you do the setup alone or with the help of a friend. I have done this for dozens of clients and I would say the average for a small business or one-person office is four hours with one person at the files and another at the computer working tandem. For larger companies with divisions and departments, the time varies. But with focus and deliberate set up, it can be done in a reasonable amount of time. Any way you look at it, the return on investment is very, very high.

Please check out this software at: www.ThePaperTiger.com

Or if you would like how the product works in real time, contact me at: Cynthia@ProPartnersInc.com with the *subject line*: **Paper Tiger**. I'll be happy to demonstrate it via screen share live on my computer. You won't be sorry.

What About Going Paperless?

An IBM employee said we would be paperless in twenty years. He said that in 1972. And now we have more paper than ever before. So it's no wonder that with this fact and with technology being what it is, going paperless seems like a feasible option. Everything is one place, it doesn't take up any physical space, and you can use the "search" feature to find anything.

Consider the approach one client took.

This client owned a lumber mill. He maintained a bank of about eight to ten four-drawer file cabinets. And one day the mill caught fire and everything—everything—burned to the ground. No paper, files, desks, or lumber was left.

When he began rebuilding the business he found much of what he wanted or needed was stored with his lawyer, accountant, and bookkeeper either in their offices or on their hard drives. So he made a radical decision.

He decided not to keep any files at his business. None. He kept current client files he was working with but everything else was tossed.

You're probably thinking he went paperless by scanning his files and putting them on a hard drive. Yes, he went paperless, but this was before technology is what it is today. So the option of scanning each document was either too expensive or not available at all. He just stopped saving paper. Period. He said all he needed that was critical was in the offices of his attorney and CPA. He was a unique kind of guy!

I'm neither advocating nor dismissing a completely paperless office. The good news is today you have more options than ever to go paperless. Technology is available that enables you to move from a paper to a completely digital system where you or a document company can maintain the information. You just need to make sure it's right for you and your business.

Keep a few things in mind:

- **Naming files** – Yes, you still need to give consideration to how the files are named and the hierarchy of your system—similar to what you would do with paper files. If you don't, clutter is waiting for you. Remember, file maintenance depends on some type of *system* to store information so you will still need to develop some naming conventions.

- **Paperless systems may have hidden costs** – Both in time and equipment. It depends on volume and budget.

Larger organizations need someone dedicated to scanning documents and assuring information goes to the correct folder. Or organizations can hire document-managing systems to do this for them. Smaller organizations can do the same thing, but resources may not be as available for the dollars and people-power required.

- **Maintenance** – If your organization scans internally, consider the costs for maintaining equipment in good working order, assuring software is current, training document management employees and auditing how well the process is working so employees can, in fact, find what they need when they need it.

- **There will still be paper** – As much as we like the idea of moving to a paperless office, paper will continue to exist. Many employees prefer working with paper so they print electronic documents. When it comes to the creative process, individuals like working with paper because it involves touching it, making notes in the margins, referring and re-reading it many times over without having to go to the computer.

Again, a paperless office is not a one-size-fits-all approach, but it's certainly something worth considering. I doubt the majority of us will ever work in a *completely* paperless office environment. It seems as humans we still like our paper.

The One Thing to Remember:

To be effective, filing systems need to be user-friendly.

Three Things You Can Do:

1. Identify no more than seven broadly named categories.

2. Name files based on how you think of them because it's about retrieving, not storing.

3. Remember that "Miscellaneous" and "Other" aren't category names. You might as well re-label them "Procrastination."

Write down *one* thing you're going to do differently or change.

The Last Word

"My filing system is messy but orderly."

Tony Benn

CHAPTER 7

Organizing *electronic* files ... Yes, I know we all have 'search'

Okay ... I really didn't know whether I should even include a chapter on setting up an electronic filing system because we all have "search" capability. So I casually asked friends to hear what they thought about including it. One person said "search on my MacBook Pro doesn't always work" or "search can get cumbersome" or "search is kind of slow."

So I sent out a survey to a broad a segment and the answer was a definite YES, please include it. Here's a comment I liked the best: "Absolutely include it! I keep everything electronically filed and because of this I can at least look at the file system and see what topics/issues/projects I have completed or am working on. Without an e-file system, I'd have no idea and also no easy way to compare documents within a file or folder." So here you have it.

Some of this is very basic information and some of it may be more than you ever wanted to know. Even if you pick up one tip helping you to save time and reduce frustration, then I'm happy. Here goes.

Step #1: Backing Up

If you're thinking of implementing any one of these suggestions, please begin with backing up what you currently have on your computer. Now. Skipping this step can cost you a lot more time and money.

There are hardware options for backing up, depending on your situation and budget, but the cost of storage—hardware or in the cloud—is very low these days. Options include an onsite server, cloud services, automated back-up services (like Mozy and Carbonite), automating backups on another external hard drive in your office, CDs, even large capacity USB drives.

There are a few types of backups to keep in mind: mirror image backups copy information to a new hard drive; file-by-file backups enable you to be more selective; incremental backups enable you to back up only what changed since the last backup; and differential backups overwrite previous versions of backup.

Step #2: Sorting Out

I'll begin this section by reminding you to always, always check with your IT department/supervisor to assure you're following policy. If you're a home-based entrepreneur or small business owner, check with your IT guy first.

If you're *cleaning out* some of your existing files, *generally* speaking you could delete .tmp or .bak files. The questions you would ask yourself are the same ones you would ask when purging a paper filing system:

- Is it financial or legal?
- Did I even know I had this file?
- Can I find it elsewhere?

If you're *archiving* information, check company policy. If you're a home-based or small business, keeping documents is impacted by financial and legal requirements, and insurance rules vary by state. So check with your attorney, CPA, and insurance broker before doing anything drastic!

If you're *removing programs*, again, check with IT and company policy.

Step #3: Organizing and Naming Files

The following diagrams will help you see how you can organize your files to make them more user-friendly.

I'll be using my own experience when I first decided to organize my hard drive many moons ago.
In Microsoft, master folders are organized alphabetically and can look something like this:

Desktop
Downloads
Music
My Documents

The default for saving documents you create is the master folder "My Documents." But that never really worked for me so I created my own master folder and my hard drive looked like this:

Desktop
Downloads
Drivers
Music
My Documents
PPI (for Productivity Partners Inc.)

I use PPI quite a bit and it seemed to be buried toward the bottom of this tree so I forced it to the top of the master files list by simply putting the number one in front of it:

1PPI
Desktop
Downloads
Drivers
Music
My Documents

Next, I made sure I didn't go more than three levels deep **(bolded below)** from my master folder. When you do, it tends to make the system more cumbersome and difficult:

> 1PPI (master folder)
>> Administrative folder (**subfolder/category**)
>>> Forms (**nested files**)
>>>> Organizing assessment (**data file**)

I'm sorting by grouping similar things together by subject, (not application).

Then I began identifying and creating no more than seven broad-based subfolders/categories (**bolded** below). You'll remember this from the previous chapter on managing paper files. Seven is the magic number and it works really great with digital files. My master folder started looking like this:

> 1PPI (master folder)
>> **Administrative folder** (subfolder/category)
>>> Forms (nested files)
>>>> Organizing assessment (data file)
>> **Client's folder** (sub-folder/category)
>>> Corporate
>>>> ABC Co.
>>>> DEF Co.
>>> Government
>>>> GHI
>>>> JKL
>>> Non Profit
>>>> MNO
>>>> PQR
>> **Marketing**
>> **Personal**
>> **Products**
>> **Services**
>> **Training**

It's really important to stop here and answer a question I get asked a lot: Do you need to match the names of your *electronic* file folders to your *paper* file folders?

Short answer: No. In fact, I wouldn't suggest it.

Not only is it difficult to maintain this over the long haul, but your brain doesn't really like it because your brain thinks differently when retrieving paper vs. digital files. The only client I ever had who was successful at this had a double Ph.D. and J.D. And that's just about what it takes to be able to maintain this approach.

However, the names of your e-mail folders can match your hard drive folders because they're both digital. It can work, but it's not a requirement.

Naming Files

I'm going to try and not confuse you with too much detail here, but there are many, many ways you can name your files in order to find them. Whatever method you choose, *be consistent* and *logical*. The approach is to identify how you normally think of files when you go to retrieve them.

Here are some examples:

For *financial* files, you can use the year and then the month:

- 0715 bank statements = July 2015
- 1015 bank statements = October 2015

For *documents* you can try just about anything, but as an example, if you retrieve by client name, you could do this:

- Jones letter 0815.docx
- Jones letter 1115.docx

If you tend to retrieve using *dates*, it could look like this:

- 0815 letter Jones.docx
- 1115 letter Jones.docx

One day I looked at my photo/image files and realized they were pretty jumbled up. For some reason I think of these types of files differently, but that's just me. So I went back in tried being more *consistent* and *logical* in how I named them. I settled on one-word descriptions when I could (desk, desk 1, desk 2, etc.), so if I used search I could find all of the same kind of image under that name.

This type of naming conventions are really about how you think of something when you go to *retrieve* it. Name? Date? City? Just remain consistent and logical in your approach and you'll probably end up with a more user-friendly filing system.

Step #4: Streamlining

If you've gotten this far, congrats! If you've found one thing you can use to help you save time and energy, great. Now let's streamline your system.

I said earlier that I used a one in front my PPI master folder in order to move it to the top of the tree. Here's another trick I picked up: When I saved my Word or Excel documents, they were saved to the original master default folder—My Documents. But to save time, I wanted the files to automatically be saved to *my* master file default-1PPI. So I went into each program and changed the default setting to save to **1PPI**.

If you want to do this and you're using Windows 10, for Windows or Excel documents you go to:

- File
- Options (bottom of left column)
- Save

GET ORGANIZED. GET FOCUSED. GET MOVING.

- Default File Location – Change from whatever is showing to the name of your master file

Now whenever I save a document, it automatically pulls up my master file—1PPI—as a starting point.

Step #5: Maintaining Your Electronic Filing System

Regular maintenance includes:

- Backing up files on a regular basis – Frequency depends on your comfort level

- Archiving – Yearly

- Deleting unnecessary files – Yearly

What About a Filing System for E-mail?

I get asked this question quite a bit. The answer to this is the same as it is with paper. Have no more than seven broad-named categories, with as many subfolders below each as you want/need.

Over the years I've received feedback from many clients telling me they've used the system for ages and it really works for them. If you maintain no more than seven categories, when you go to retrieve something your brain only has seven choices and not fifty-plus, which is what I normally see.

Broad-named categories include names such as Administrative, Financial, HR, Marketing, Sales, Personal, etc.

Another question I get asked is about how long to save or how to approach purging an e-mail filing system. Well ... here's my story. Years and years ago I got a new computer, and in the process of transferring information from the old one to the new one the e-mail filing cabinet didn't transfer. It was lost. Completely. Minor concern set in because I thought for sure I'd need something I'd lost in the transfer. More than five years went by and not once did I ever need that lost information.

Fast forward many years later and it happened ... again. I transferred computers and all e-mail files were lost again. It's been years and I've never missed one of those files. So because of this experience, my e-mail files are pretty minimal.

The Pareto Principle applies to paper and electronic files. The statistic says 80% of what we file we never look at again. I've done informal research over the years with clients and it seems to be true. Between 75-80% are never looked at again.

The One Thing to Remember:

Filing is about retrieving, not storing information.

Three Things You Can Do:

1. Identify no more than seven broad-named categories.

2. Name files based on how you think of them because it's about retrieving, not storing.

3. Remember that "Miscellaneous" and "Other" aren't category names. You might as well relabel them "Procrastination."

Write down *one* thing you're going to do differently or change.

The Last Word

Fifty-six percent of respondents claim to spend thirty minutes a week "looking for files they cannot find" on their computer.

More than 33% say they "somewhat" or "very" often must spend time reprinting previously created documents because they have been misplaced.

P-Touch Survey, 2010

CHAPTER 8

Keeping and letting go of paper

As I mentioned earlier in the book, a full four-drawer filing cabinet contains 18,000 pieces of paper, and more keeps coming. So unless we learn to let go of paper we're forced to keep requesting additional filing cabinets or hard drive space—both of which are, on many levels, costly. Price Waterhouse said an average organization:

- Makes nineteen copies of each document

- Spends $20 in labor to file each document

- Spends $120 in labor searching for each misfiled document

- Loses one out of every twenty documents

- Spends twenty-five hours recreating each lost documents

I haven't even seen the stats on the cost of electronic file clutter and time spent, but I suspect they're interesting!

Archiving

If you work for a larger organization – your company may already have policies and procedures about how long paper and electronic information can be kept before it's shredded or permanently deleted. Your first step is to check with your supervisor or legal department to understand these policies regarding document retention.

If you're a small business owner – costs involved with maintaining information systems are an even bigger consideration for the small business owner. If you want to be really productive, call your accountant and legal advisor and find out if/what the financial and legal requirements are for your business and set up a system supporting these requirements. This will include categories, subcategories, naming conventions, archiving rules, and destruction rules so all employees know how information is handled in your company.

If you're a one-person shop – it's all up to you and your accountant and attorney. Follow the same suggestions I made for a small business owner.

Listed below is a *general* retention system cheat sheet for personal files. As always, check with your financial and legal advisors before discarding any document as requirements may vary from state to state.

For company files, check with the person in your organization authorized for providing this information:

Records to keep SEVEN YEARS OR MORE:

- ❏ Brokerage and fund transactions showing a "buy" and/or "sell" transaction

- ❏ Certificates of Deposit

- ❏ House records including deed and cancelled checks for capital improvements

- ❑ Insurance policies

- ❑ Partnership agreements (K-1s)

- ❑ Retirement Plan documentation (IRAs, KEOGHs, SEPs)

- ❑ Receipts for major purchases

- ❑ Stock-option agreements

- ❑ Tax records

Records to keep ALL YOUR LIFE:

Agreements
- Alimony
- Custody
- Prenuptial
- Trust

Certificates
- Birth
- Death
- Divorce Decrees
- List of financial assets *and* advisors
- Medical Records

Papers
- Military
- Naturalization
- Power of attorney
- Video recording of valuables

- Wills
- Your W-2 statements

Letting Go

Letting go of paper can be more difficult for some people than others. I'm not talking about memorabilia or personal items, but business documents.

When you decide to begin a project to purge paper, here are some questions you can ask yourself to hopefully make it a bit easier:

1. **Is the document legal or financial?** If so, it generally lives under a specific set of deletion rules. Sometimes this also includes technical or research-oriented documents. Check with your accountant and attorney.

2. **Did you even know you had the document?** Let's face it—if you didn't even know you had the document, what value is it bringing you? If you didn't know it was part of your 18,000 pieces of paper or megabyte of information on your hard drive, consider letting go of it. It's taking up precious space, and why take the time to keep revisiting every time you clean out your cabinets?

3. **Do I think I'll need this *someday*?** Warning—whenever you hear yourself say "someday" it's usually a road toward procrastination and stuffed filing cabinets. Unless you have a solid reason and timeline for using information, it might be best to consider getting rid of it. Because of the speed of business and technology today, so much of what we keep—and find later—has become obsolete. So unless you have definite plans, consider letting go of that file or document.

This is not an exhaustive list and some of these questions may not resonate with you so feel free to develop your own—anything that will help you get to an effective "yes" or "no" answer.

Some Guidelines to Consider

1. **Clean out your files 2x/year** – If you plan on twice a year, maybe you might only get to it once a year which is the minimum. Put a cleanout date on your calendar during a time of year that isn't busy for you or your business. I do mine the last week of the year. If you wait and only do this every five years, the task just becomes harder and takes longer.

   Companies and departments in larger organizations should consider having an annual "Clean Out Your Files" day—paper or electronic. Make it fun and worthwhile.

2. **Find a Toss Trainer** – If you're someone who has difficulty getting rid of paper, find a Toss Trainer. This is someone who can act as a type of coach for you. This person can be a friend, family member, or teammate who is willing to work with you by standing in your office and holding the trash bag or shredding documents.

   If you begin to hesitate—as we all do—the Toss Trainer is there to encourage you and ask prompting questions to help you let go. They're there to help you keep moving forward faster.

Two Client Stories with a Similar Theme

I was working with a global organization whose offices were moving to new buildings. The new offices were half the size they were previously and everyone saw and knew these new space requirements.

I was asked to work with employees to help them pare down. Unfortunately, I was asked to work with the Marketing Department. I say unfortunately because if you've ever spent time in the Marketing Department, samples of all their work efforts abound ... everywhere. Every campaign, poster, giveaway, toy, reminder, prototype, etc. is saved and on display. So my work was cut out for me.

I worked with Janice who knew exactly why I was there and what we were working toward. For the very first piece of paper in her filing cabinet, it took ten minutes for her to make a final decision about its disposition. Ten minutes. We had several more file drawers to go so I began asking questions and I could see that making decisions was going to be difficult for her.

We made a few rules and things started to move along, but then we ran into another snag. She began running across some giveaways that reminded her of previously launched successful campaigns, previous unsuccessful campaigns, a colleague, a boss ... you get the idea. It was her history with the company that she was reliving. So some things got tossed/shredded, but there were these *other* files that were causing a problem.

At first, I suggested she take them home. She said she couldn't because her husband would kill her. He thought she already had too much stuff at home.

Then I suggested she give them to other teammates. But they didn't really want them because they had their own "stuff" to deal with.

The only other option was for her to put them in the trunk of her car and drive around with them, which of course was no option at all!

Then I realized each employee had a box in front of their office where they put things they didn't want to throw out but didn't want to keep either. Anything in the box was up for grabs for anyone interested. I suggested she put these more difficult decisions in the box for anyone interested in them so we could keep moving along. This worked for her and she began doing just that.

Whatever wasn't grabbed by someone was ultimately picked up nightly by the maintenance people. And the contents were then discarded.

What she needed was an interim step. As a type of Toss Trainer, I provided an option that worked for her to be able to let go.

Here's another example of helping someone let go of paper:

I had a small business client who owned a printing business. Alexa was a very creative person and definitely a Piler. She'd been in her current building for many years and now found herself wanting to move to much smaller offices. She had tons of papers, files, drawings, prints, posters, etc.

When we began working together, she wasn't having too much trouble with the normal paperwork. Memos, budgets, training manuals, etc. Then we got to the beautiful customized covers of calendars hanging on the walls of her office and throughout the company.

Alexa was having a very difficult time letting go of the calendars because she truly saw them as a work of art. And I could see why—some were truly beautiful.

So I stopped and asked if she could think of another use for these covers. Hanging on the walls for all these years rendered them something of a bulletin board. She barely looked at them and paid no attention to the beauty she saw when they were new. It was only when we were ready to get rid of them that it reminded her of the artist and creativity involved.

After brainstorming several ideas, we came up with the concept of donating them to a hospital or a home for the elderly so patients could use them for projects during potential rehabilitation. She seemed content with this idea and I committed to taking them to the places we identified.

We stacked the calendars in a large box and she walked me out and watched me put them in the trunk of my car, but she still wanted to grab them and run back inside. Trust me, it was a quick getaway!

Janice and Alexa were Pilers and very creative. Characteristically, this style and piling/visual retrieval seem to go hand-in-hand. From what I've seen, creatives associate things with people. Just the thought of how much work the creative piece took can overwhelm them.

I'm not talking about memorabilia or nostalgic things like a teacup that belonged to your grandmother. They recall the time, energy, and creativeness of the person who was associated with the object. They remember the friend, family, teammate, client, or customer whom they worked with so diligently on a project. This scenario is what they think of when trying to throw the object out.

You can help someone who is having this type of difficulty by providing them with an option similar to the box that was outside Janice's office. That, or the rerouting of the calendar covers for Alexa which made it easier for her to envision the life of the object after she let go.

If you're more of a Piler than a Filer, tossing out tends to be a bit more difficult for you. Look for a Toss Trainer. They can really help you continue moving forward when it comes to making those hard decisions.

The One Thing to Remember:

> Learning to let go keeps unimportant things moving out
> to make room for more important things.

Three Things You Can Do:

1. Clean out twice a year.

2. When you hear yourself say "someday," beware that you might be on the road to delaying a decision.

3. Find the right Toss Trainer.

Write down *one* thing you're going to do differently or change.

The Last Word

*"What the world really needs
is more love and less paperwork."*

Pearl Bailey, Singer

CHAPTER 9

Management, maintenance, and motivation

Getting organized requires some deliberate and diligent actions on your part. It's easy to feel discouraged and begin to feel like it's hopeless.

Not true.

You just need to remember to take a big project and break it down into smaller, manageable pieces, one bite at a time.

There are several things you can do toward creating a system that you can easily use, manage, and maintain.

I use the formula **SPM**. It means:

> **S**et up a system
> **P**ractice your processes
> **M**anage your behavior

Set Up a System

Based on the information you've read, here are some questions to ask yourself when setting up an office system:

Do I ...

- Understand how work flows through my office?

- Have a home base for incoming information?

- Have an Office Road Map for a U-shaped or L-shaped desk layout?

- Have a Desk Road Map and clearly understand the four levels of access within my office space?

- Do I know my style of paper management? Am I a Piler, Filer, or Combo?

- Know how to set up my system to accommodate my style?

- Know what I need/want to do to set up a user-friendly filing system?

Got it? Great. If not, take the time to set your system and foundation and revisit those areas challenging you.

Practice Your Processes

Based on the information you've read, here are some questions to ask yourself when it comes to practicing your processes:

Am I ...

- Able to handle today's mail today?

- Storing my incoming information in its home base on a regular basis? (Stacking my deck)

- Practicing the first level sort by using the AFTR approach? (Dealing the cards)

- Practicing the second level sort by further dividing my information into actions I need to take by asking *what is the very next thing that has to happen* to this?

- Tweaking my desktop storage system according to what feels comfortable and loosely based on my style?

- Developing a paper and electronic filing system ... or finding a system?

Got it? Great. If not, take the time to set your foundation and revisit the process you find challenging.

Manage Your Behavior

Not always the easiest thing to do.

Based on the information in this book, here are some questions to ask yourself when it comes to managing and maintaining your organizing behavior.

Do I ...

- Consistently place incoming information in its home base?

- Try to handle today's mail today, and if I can't, do I have backup plan?

- Review my file pile on a regular basis through a calendar reminder I've set up?

- File information away on a regular basis through a calendar reminder I've set up?

- Do I clear out my filing cabinets at least 2x/year based on a calendar reminder I've set up?

- Need or have I identified a Toss Trainer to help me in the process of cleaning out my filing system or letting go of paper/information?

If you're struggling with these questions go back and review chapters that apply to your particular challenge. That being said, now is a good time to remind you that organizing systems can and need to change according to what is happening in your world. They're more dynamic than static, so small tweaks along the way are a good thing to support your systems and processes.

So if your current system is working and something at work changes, take time to step back and think through the situation to see what you need to set up in your system that might be different than what you needed before.

You might find that it will require just moving or adding something rather than getting involved in an entire organizational overhaul. The key is to remain conscious of the requirements of the new situation and set up an organizing system that supports you and the demands of your new situation.

Just remember: How do you eat an elephant? One bite at a time.

The One Thing to Remember:

> Your situation didn't get this way overnight and it won't be solved overnight. It takes time and commitment.

Three Things You Can Do:

Try not to underestimate the ...

1. Amount of time it takes to set up the *initial* system.

2. Amount of work it will take *without interruption*.

3. *Number of things* that compete for your attention.

Write down *one* thing you're going to do differently or change.

The Last Word

"The secret of change is to focus all of your energy not on fighting the old, but on building the new."

Unknown

SECTION 2:
INTRODUCTION

Time Management

Organizing is part of time management—a big, important part, but still only part of a much bigger picture.

Now I want to talk about your time management so you can continue to work toward improving your performance, productivity, and peace of mind.

The Center for Brain Health at the University of Texas at Dallas suggests doing these four things to keep your mind alert during the day:

1. Rest your brain by quieting it a few times each day.

2. Refrain from multi-tasking and focus on one task at a time.

3. Prioritize your daily to-do list.

4. Try new things and not same old, same old.

In this section of the book I'll talk a lot about the first three. Let's start with your time management **GPS**.

Goals
Priorities
Schedules

I'll also talk about the types of things that interfere with your GPS. These include:

- Poor communications

- Failing to set boundaries

- Procrastination

- Micromanaging

Just like your car's GPS, if you don't pay attention to these or you take a wrong turn, you'll have to reroute. And as we all know, rerouting causes precious loss of time, money, and stress. So put your seatbelt on and let's go for a spin.

CHAPTER 10

Your time management GPS: Goals

Of all the subjects on time management I really think this is the one area written about the most. Most of the information we see is around the end of the calendar year when employees are determining their business goals for the following year. However, developing goals, especially personal ones, can be done at any time.

Dr. Gary Latham has spent many years researching the issue of goal setting and has identified many types of goals including outcome, learning, proximal, superordinate, and participative. Whew.

What I'll talk about here are goals tied to either your company or your personal life, because we need both. Without goals, we can lack ...

Challenge
Accomplishment
Meaning
Focus
Determined action
Persistent action
Clarity
Strategies for work and life

So you see why goals are both important and a key element when moving toward more effective management of your time. Yet many people still struggle with developing and setting goals. I think part of the reason there's so much information out there is because of three things we tend to do.

First, we don't really know the secret to successfully identifying a real goal, so we write something—or anything—down. This is a matter of learning.

Second, we might believe that a goal is a win/lose proposition at any point in its cycle. This is a matter of education.

Third, if we fail to get where we want, we tend to throw up our hands and say, "See, I knew I couldn't do it." This is a matter of learning to set goals that work for you and not against you!

In my goal setting classes I share a four-step process. I call it "See it, Own it, Set it, Get it."

Step 1: See It

If you've ever been involved in a strategic planning process or started your own company you know that this type of planning builds a foundation. It includes long-term goals that are reviewed and revisited annually. One of the things you do during the session is identify the company's vision—what is it shooting to become or do?

This approach isn't much different for individuals. It's important to be able to see yourself in the future and have a vision of what you want to accomplish. It can be big or it can be small, but it needs to be realistic for you. Maybe you want to be ...

> Healthier
> Richer
> Smarter
> More mindful
> More successful
> More social
> More spiritual

You get the idea. It's a new, more positive version of you.
So your first step is to identify what you *want to be*.

Once you have that vision, it's time to write down the goal. Don't let it just be something that rattles around in your head. Write it down and keep it where you can see it as a reminder of what you want and need to happen.

Most of us are familiar with the S.M.A.R.T. acronym that says goals need to have five characteristics:

> Smart
> Measurable
> Attainable
> Relevant
> Timeline

Whether you use this acronym or not, remember that the more vague your goals are, the less likely you'll reach them. So when you write down your goal, make sure it is very specific and has a deadline. Want to test it? When you reach the deadline you set forth, you should be able to answer the question of whether or not you made your goal with a "yes" or "no" response.

Step 2: Own It

For me, this is the most important step. It's the one that's most often missed. Why? Because frequently I hear people feel they need to have a goal just to, well, have one. Or they write it down and make it specific and clear and think that's enough. Or worse yet, they've written a goal because somebody else said they should. The component that determines whether or not you actually make your goal a reality is *how you feel about it*—whether or not you identify with a desire to make and meet the goal.

> Does it motivate you?
> Do you own it *emotionally*?
> Is this the right time to work on it?

If the answer to these types of questions is "no" then let go of the goal until you're ready for it. Trying to force it not only doesn't work but can leave you feeling more discouraged than if you never had one to begin with.

Let me share a personal story.

In the past, I'd never been one for daily exercise even though I know how good it is for you. Sure, I'd play tennis, golf, and swim, but when it came to a daily routine I always found a reason not to do it. I'd say it's boring, it's not fun, I won't get the results I want, it's expensive, etc. Any excuse to *not* do it seemed to work. And then my mother became ill.

I knew that caring for her would take all my emotional strength and physical energy and I still had a business to run, a house to maintain, as well as other family members who needed me. I realized if I didn't take care of myself she would suffer.

So I thought about what type of exercise program I could get into to manage the level of stress that was already visiting me—something that would work for my type of schedule and demands, and I came up with a walking program.

I decided a walking would be best because all I really needed was a good pair of walking shoes. But I also needed someplace to shield me from the freezing cold winds of winter and blazing hot summers. Then I remembered I lived close to a large mall.

Great. Now I had plan. But even at this point I was already beginning to question my success. Not a good sign.

Here's what happened.

I began my walking program in the winter with plans to get up no later than 5:45 a.m. The only time I've really gotten up that early is to catch a plane. But that's what I had to do. More doubt set in. Nevertheless, I began.

The alarm clock went off and for the first couple days I just rolled over and stayed in my nice warm bed. Then on the third day I asked myself *why* I kept putting it off. Why did I want to do this to begin with? Then I remembered. If something happened to me because of the stress and demands of being a caregiver, then something would happen to the people I loved.

So the next morning I got up and went to the mall and walked.

I did it again and again until the end of the week. And then the next week and next month and next year. It eventually became a habit that I've continued five days a week for the past seven years.

The key here is that I originally felt I *had* to do this until I realized I *wanted* to do this because I loved my family and the consequences or outcome of not doing it was too great.

Cue the "ah-ha" light.

I was truly motivated by my goal because I connected to it emotionally. I owned it. It was mine.

Step 3: Set It

Getting up at 5:45 a.m. and walking five days a week didn't just automatically happen. I needed to get ready mentally and physically and recognize the triggers that could help or prevent me from achieving doing this. I needed a checklist and an action plan of some sort.

- First, I needed good walking shoes.

- Second, any excuse could trigger me to think about not walking so I eliminated as many roadblocks as I could by making sure my shoes and clothes were laid out the night before. A visual reminder always helps me.

- Third, I learned out how long one turn around the mall was (3/4 of a mile) and decided when I would increase the distance or time.

- Fourth, I figured if I was going to walk I was going to see if it helped my health, so I scheduled an appointment with the doctor to get a baseline.

I set my expectations as realistically as I could and knew that these four things needed to happen.

If you have a vision for becoming more organized and less stressed and your goal is to have that happen in a couple weekends, you're probably setting an unrealistic expectation for yourself and that usually throws a monkey wrench in the works. Revisit your plan and approach to make sure you're setting realistic expectations.

Step 4: Get It

This part of goal setting really has to do with tracking and measuring. You need timelines and milestones in order to review your progress. However, don't fall into a common trap.

The trap is thinking that if the results aren't what you want, it's time to stop or give up because you think you can't get there. The truth is that the tracking and measurement can and should be motivators and not de-motivators. They let you know where you stand and what you might need to adjust.

Why? Because goals should be just slightly outside your reach. You can see them, you can feel them, and you can almost touch them. If they're set miles and miles away you can lose impetus. So setting and resetting goals to realistic measures is what helps keep them as something that motivates you rather than seeing them as a devastating self-judgment on poor progress.

For example, let's say you set a goal to walk a certain number of miles a day/week, but you broke your toe. That doesn't mean you need to give up your goal; you may just have to adjust the timeframe for miles walked. Or try a different exercise for a while until you mend. If goals end up either too aggressive or beyond your control, by all means, revise them and track your progress. As the saying goes, no reason to "throw the baby out with the bathwater."

How Many Goals?

The number of goals you set for yourself is important because we tend to set *too many*. The ideal is to have one major work-related goal and one major personal-related goal. The more you identify, the more your brain tends to overload, lose focus, and disengage. Remember, long-term goals take time and usually many steps to achieve. When it comes to goals it's really about the *quality* and not the quantity that matters.

The One Thing to Remember:

If you don't emotionally connect to your goal(s), anything and everything will become a distraction that prevents you from achieving it.

Three Things You Can Do:

1. If your goal isn't motivating you, take a minute to ask why. It may mean simply rewording it with a finer point to make it sing for you.

2. Make sure the goal is specific and clear so on the deadline date you will be able to answer the question "Did I make my goal?" with a "yes" or "no."

3. Revisit goals on a monthly basis and make small revisions as needed. Small adjustments help keep your expectations adjusted and your spirit motivated.

Write down *one* thing you're going to do differently or change.

The Last Word

"Vision without execution is hallucination."

Thomas Edison

CHAPTER 11

Your time management GPS: Prioritizing

Most of us know what priority means. It means the *single most* important thing.

You have more than one priority, but it's ineffective to think you can work on more than one at a time. Picking the one you need to work on means it's the most important thing you need to be doing at that moment. Doing this consistently and routinely is what moves your goal(s) forward.

I always think it's helpful to see a visual representation of how we divide our time, so here's a little history.

Before Dwight Eisenhower became President, he was a General in the military and also commander of the Allied Forces in Europe during WWII. He was known to have exceptional planning skills and a "tight rein" on his time. At one point he developed a visual tool to help military leaders make decisions. This tool became known as the Eisenhower Box and it looked like this:

	URGENT	NOT URGENT
IMPORTANT	Do	Decide
NOT IMPORTANT	Delegate	Delete

He is quoted as having said, "What is important is seldom urgent and what is urgent is seldom important." And his diagram shows that quite simply.

Decades later in the seventies, Stephen Covey used the Eisenhower Box to create what has since become known as the Covey Matrix. Instead of military interventions, however, Covey was concerned about how all the technology being developed would cause people to lose sight of their priorities and take time from their families. He wanted to be able to demonstrate his theory and provide people a visual representation, so he used the quadrants below. The emphasis was to stay above the middle horizontal line.

Quadrant I was urgent + important.
Quadrant II was not urgent + important.
Quadrant III was urgent + not important
Quadrant IV was not urgent + not important.

Covey Matrix

	URGENT	NOT URGENT
IMPORTANT	QI Crisis Last Minute Deadlines Production Issues	QII Priorities Relationship Building Planning New Opportunities
NOT IMPORTANT	QIII Interruptions Some Meetings Some E-mail	QIV Busy Work Computer Games Various Time-wasters

When Covey wrote his books, he shared some guidelines about how much of your time should be spent in each quadrant in order to be effective.

Quadrant I   15%
Quadrant II   75%
Quadrant III   9%
Quadrant IV   1%

Fast forward three-plus decades to see how we really spend our time.

The book entitled 5 *Choices: The Practical Path to Extraordinary Productivity* by Kogon, Merrill, and Rinne was published in January 2015. In the book, the authors reference a six-year global study that showed how people spend their time *today*. And here's how those percentages played out in this day and age:

    Quadrant I   27.6%
    Quadrant II   30.8%
    Quadrant III   23.6%
    Quadrant IV   17.9%

In addition, they analyzed the picture and found people were spending:

    51.2% of their time on *urgent* matters
    41.5% of their time on *unimportant things*
    And only 30.8% of their time on *things that really mattered.*

Eye-opener, isn't it? But perhaps not so surprising to today's workforce.

I've had my business since 1992 and over the course of time I've heard and seen how the shift in identifying and working on priorities has happened ... slowly, but steadily.

In the early nineties, employees were saying they weren't really clear on what their priorities were. Then Stephen Covey and his body of work came along and helped people identify their personal and professional priorities.

Fast forward another decade and employees said yes, they could identify their priorities, but they didn't always tether them to their goals. This type of disconnect caused confusion and resulted in less productivity, not more.

Fast forward to the past ten years or so and I've seen another shift.

Today, employees tell me they know what's important and understand how moving toward the goal daily is critical, but most days *they simply can't get to their priorities* due to the current 24/7 business demands and expectations.

I really think there are two issues that sidetrack you from working on priorities on a regular basis.

First, company priorities keep shifting, sometimes from minute to minute. What was important to do when you left your house for the office this morning has changed by the time you get there, and it may change again by noon or the end of the day. Being agile helps an organization remain competitive in today's business climate, so flexing and shifting are almost a requirement. This presents its own set of challenges for employees.

Second, the way we get off track varies. There are internal and external reasons that I've termed *priority potholes*. These include poor or ineffective communications, not being able to say no, procrastination, delegating ineffectively and being disorganized to name a few. How does most of this happen? Through technology (the savior and the culprit) and other human beings. I'll cover these topics in later chapters.

But the bottom line is that for the most part you can control your outcomes by controlling your approach. The way you think and what you do. This involves a couple things.

Since being consistent in working on your priorities is what moves goals forward, it stands to reason that your goal(s) need to be clear and resonate with you, as I talked about in the previous chapter. Your goal needs to be purposeful with some emotional power under it. If that's not clear, then the reason for working on your priority—rather than something that seems urgent—becomes very foggy. When that happens, anything and everything will interfere with priority work.

If you want to remember what's important in life, take some time to read the book *Crazy Busy* by Dr. Edward M. Hallowell—the same man who co-authored *Driven to Distraction*, which is about ADHD. He makes a great case in an interesting way of reminding us of what we seem to have stepped away from in the years since technology has become such a big part of our lives.

The One Thing to Remember:

Priorities are always connected to your goal.

Three Things You Can Do:

1. Work on your priority first, every morning, before you do anything else.

2. Set up rituals to cue you into taking action, and those actions will become habits.

3. Shifting priorities are the norm, so throughout the day try asking yourself, "Is this the most important thing I need to be working on right now?"

Write down *one* thing you're going to do differently or change.

The Last Word

*"The main thing is to keep
the main thing the main thing."*

Stephen Covey

CHAPTER 12

Your time management GPS: Scheduling and planning

Scheduling

If you've spent time with your goals and identified your priorities, scheduling time to work on them is the next step.

Sometimes that's easier said than done for the reasons I've outlined in previous chapters. Nonetheless, without putting it "on the books," it tends not to happen.

The Question About To-Do Lists

Let's take step back. Let's say you've identified something or many things you need to do. You've created a to-do list. If there is one question I get asked almost every day, it's "What type of to-do list do you maintain?" or "What app do you use?" My answer may surprise you.

I don't maintain a daily to-do list, and I don't use an app.

I did once in my life, early in my career, before technology came along. I carried a pad of paper where I listed things I needed to do and crossed them off as I went along. Whatever didn't get done that day got transferred to the next piece of paper for the next day. Ancient history.

However, this isn't ancient history for everyone. Some clients still need and want paper to capture either their daily to-dos or the thoughts, ideas, and concepts that run across their mind during the day. They feel that technology isn't either fast or convenient enough, or they forget what's in their phone/tablet. They need to see and connect to the visual presence of a list. And for this group, I have a suggestion.

In the previous chapter I talked about the Eisenhower Box and the Covey Matrix. I've grown rather fond of these tools and now believe just about anything can be determined by using a quadrant as a visual. I've become the Quadrant Queen.

Eventually, my to-do list evolved into *quadrants* rather than a long list. It looked something like this:

Things I Need To Do

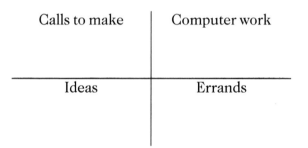

Why did I do this? In Chapter 3 I talked about the importance of *sorting* papers because it begins creating a structure you could use day in and day out. The quadrants sort and group similar activities together. So at the end of the day I would tear this piece of paper out and do what I needed to do based on the groupings.

As archaic as this may sound, it worked. And it still works for some of my clients today—even highly successful ones who never found a way to identify, sort, or transfer information to actionable outcomes. Some take the information and put it into their calendar or other electronic files, but the initial collection of the information happens with pen and paper in a quadrant format. Research has proven that writing something down improves cognitive learning. If paper and pen work for you, that's all that matters.

So how do I remember what to do if I don't maintain a daily to-do list or use an app?

Things that I need to do go directly into my electronic calendar.

What? Why?

Because in my case, my calendar drives me—I live in it! Without it I'm totally lost, and I've worked with many others who use their calendar the same way.

So here's my point: It's never a one-size-fits-all approach. It's not always paper or electronic or long lists that help. It's what works for *you*.

Long-term To-Do Lists

There is one type of list that I DO maintain—a list of projects that are more strategic in nature that I've identified as either important or worth exploring. These projects tend to take time and not just an hour or two of research. They usually involve several steps and may or may not be do-able during the current year but could be worked on the following year or a few years out. I call this my **Main Brain**.

If you've read this far you know I like quadrants as a way to sort and prioritize, so my Main Brain is divided into quadrants and it looks like this:

Main Brain

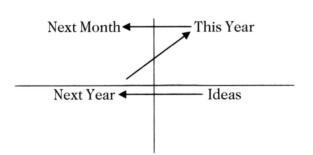

Here's How My Main Brain Works for Me

I went into my electronic calendar and created a recurring event on the fourth Tuesday of the month. The event is labeled Main Brain. I add things there as they occur in my "other" brain—the one between my ears.

On the fourth Tuesday of the month I do what my calendar says which is look at my Main Brain quadrants. If I can't manage to do this on that day I schedule it for another day *that same week*. It's important because it keeps both my business and me moving forward so I try not to ignore it.

I look at my Main Brain and review if there's something I need to add, delete, or move in my quadrants. If something moves to the Next Month quadrant, I see where it will work on my calendar for the following month. If there are multiple steps to something I need or want to do, I identify the first step and put it on my calendar. If I decide I'm not ready yet, then I let the item stay where it is.

All of this really doesn't take very long, but this tool helps me with planning my route. And this planning process is hitched to my **goal(s)** and **priorities.**

The best thing about using the quadrants this way is that I found software that lets me add and modify tasks and move them from one quadrant to another through 'drag and drop' actions. It's called Priority Matrix software that enables you to sync your tasks/priorities with your teammates. However, I find it flexible enough to use the quadrants any way I want. So for me it works to securely capture my strategic thoughts and make sure the actions connected to them keep moving forward all the way to landing on my calendar.

But you could also simply have a piece of paper with four columns that look like this:

1.   First column: Ideas

2. Second column: Next Year

3. Third column: This Year

4. Fourth column: Next Month

Electronically, you can cut and paste something from the first column to the second, the third to the fourth, etc.

From fourth column you populate your calendar with all or parts of the project.

We all get caught up in the day-to-day of our lives. My Main Brain has saved me from forgetting what's important in the long run when my "Other" brain is tired, overwhelmed, or just plain forgets!

Four Things to Consider When Scheduling:

First, you want to minimize the stress involved. So if you think something is going to take ten minutes, give it twenty. If you think it's going to take you thirty minutes to get somewhere, give yourself forty-five minutes to an hour. Building some cushion time in your schedule is more realistic and a lot less stressful that cutting it down to the wire. Who needs more stress?

Second, don't just delete something you had scheduled for yourself to do because of an emergency or something else that came along. If you put it in your calendar to begin with, it was probably important. Just find another time that week to reschedule it—because it's important and needs to happen, especially if it's one of your strategic goals.

Third, make sure your software syncs across all devices. This may seem obvious, but I frequently need to remind employees that unless this happens, all your potential improved productivity is lost.

Fourth, if you don't want to use technology for calendaring, then don't. There are still plenty of people out there who would prefer doing their calendar with paper, and there's nothing wrong with that. It may not be the fastest or most productive way to maintain your day, but it needs to work for you and no one else.

Planning

My original to-do list, my electronic calendar, and my Main Brain represent tools and methodologies that work for me, and I'm confident you can find an approach with tools that work for you as well. But all of this requires planning. Which requires focus. Which requires some quiet time. And that's something we really need to carve out for ourselves, because it doesn't just happen. In fact, researcher Dr. Edward Hallowell says, "Modern office life and an increasingly common condition called attention deficit trait are turning steady executives into frenzied underachievers."

However, there are plenty of people who simply don't want to plan or see the value of taking time to do so. Take my cousin, for example.

My cousin isn't much of a planner. He likes to just "do." It seems to be a bit of a family trait. So when he bought a grill and decided he would take the time to put it together, rather than paying someone else to do it or asking a buddy to help, I got a bit concerned. My suggestions on saving time aren't always thought of as wonderful, but I thought it was worth mentioning that five minutes of *planning* it out might save him thirty minutes of *doing*. I've tracked this with clients and I find it to be true. My suggestion didn't really work and he moved onward.

He begins. He puts all the pieces out on the floor. He's never done this before, but he doesn't want to take the time to read instructions. No plan—he just feels he can "figure it out" along the way. Okay. I'm sure you can figure out the rest.

Four hours later, there are parts left over, the grill is lopsided, there's frustration and a few hungry people. The grill ultimately ended up being disassembled and taken back to the store where he paid for someone to put it together. Of course, there was frustration on his part, but there was also a loss of time that he'll never get back.

Here's a really simple example of how planning can help:

Back in 1994, when my business was new, I read a book by Dr. Eugene Griessman called *Time Tactics of Very Successful People.* Today you can find dozens and dozens of posts about what successful people do to be more productive, but back then the subject wasn't that common.

One thing I read which stuck with me forever was truly simple, but I just never thought about it.

One person in the book decided to plan his weekly shopping and errands by determining which side of the street certain stores were on. He planned his route accordingly. When gas was is $5/gallon, this strategy saves money. It also saves time by simplifying the number of turns you have to make and enabling you to go with the flow of the traffic. I use it to this day.

So planning how and when you want to work on your priorities is the first step to actually scheduling them. So now it's time to schedule.

I began this chapter by saying if you've spent time with your goals and identified your priorities then scheduling time to work on them is the next step. Just remember to put some planning muscle behind it to increase your chance of success.

And Don't Forget Your Body's Rhythms

There is plenty of evidence that proves your body has circadian rhythms in which it works best, and neuroscience tells us that the same is true of your brain. It has moments and times where peak productivity is possible. The trick is in defining those times for yourself. We all get caught up in the business of our workday, but if you can determine when those peak mind and body periods are for you, you will have a powerful advantage in keeping your thinking clear and focused.

The One Thing to Remember:

Five minutes of planning saves thirty minutes of doing.

Three Things You Can Do:

1. Try keeping things you need to do in your calendar, rather than a to-do list.

2. Break large activities into smaller, bite-sized pieces.

3. Do the thing you dislike most—first. Get it out of the way.

Write down *one* thing you're going to do differently or change.

The Last Word

*"Even if you are on the right track,
you will get run over if you just sit there."*

Will Rogers

CHAPTER 13

Productivity Pothole #1: E-mail, texts, instant messaging, meetings, and one-on-one communications

"What we have here is a failure to communicate."

This is a famous line from the 1967 movie *Cool Hand Luke* starring Paul Newman and George Kennedy. When the movie was in its heyday, that sentence was repeated over and over again in the halls of corporate America and you can probably guess why. From time to time I still use it in a training, because, as the saying goes, "It's all about communicating, isn't it?"

What I've heard and learned along the way is that many problems stem from ineffective communications or lack thereof. This is true whether it's one-on-one, one to a group, phone or voice-mail, text or e-mail, or a simple written piece of paper. As a productivity strategist, my main concern is how poor or ineffective communication impacts an employee's job performance. And there's plenty of evidence that says it does.

E-mail, E-mail, E-mail

Yes. E-mail. Can you relate to the picture?

We're getting more than ever before. The average number of e-mails received a day by my clients is seventy-five, and this figure doesn't include instant messaging or texts. And it's not slowing down any time soon. So let's talk about it. Here's some interesting information I ran across when working on a webinar:

- The Bush Administration turned over more than 100 million e-mails to the National Archives—more than three times the volume from the Clinton Administration.

- The world's first e-mail sent between two computers was sent in 1971.

- Queen Elizabeth II was the first head of state to send an e-mail in 1976. (*Source: Office Solutions*)

- John Paul II became the first pope to send an e-mail apology. (*Source: Wall Street Journal, 3/5/07*)

- Thirty-seven percent of respondents were unclear about what constitutes an official business record versus a casual e-mail. (*Source: ePolicy Institute survey*)

- Of 840 U.S. businesses surveyed, twenty percent had e-mails subpoenaed. (*Source: AMA survey*)

The last two items on this list are worrisome. There are serious financial and legal implications for a company whose employees aren't clear about what a business document actually is and how it can be used for and against a company.

E-mail was originally intended to be a brief and specific communication between two individuals. Today e-mail is used as an inbox, a to-do list, a filing system, and a database.

I see it every day: Professional organizers know that clutter on the desktop can equate to clutter in the hard drive. And those are major stressors and productivity potholes. Clients always wish and think I have a bulletproof approach, secret sauce, or magic wand to help them fix this problem. I don't.

What to do?

Incoming E-mail

First, admit that you have very limited control over how many e-mails a day you receive.

Yes, we can ask our name be removed from distribution lists, unsubscribe, create spam filters, and use apps such as unroll.me, but what about the ones we get from other employees?

In larger organizations, e-mail distribution lists just grow and grow. And a lot of it is because someone thinks it's a good idea to add your name to the sender list. But I've learned that a bigger part of it is that in the company culture it can be considered politically incorrect to ask for your name to be removed. I'm not totally clear why and I'm sure it varies from organization to organization, but if you're the one creating the distribution list, you may want to check with someone before adding their name. You may also want to make it easy for them to remove their name without any type of repercussion.

If you're a leader within the organization, consider leading the charge by identifying when or what types of topics/e-mails you would like to be included on. This not only helps you with your own productivity but also acts as a model for employees who would like to do the same thing but are struggling with how to accomplish this without stepping on toes.

Outgoing E-mail

Okay, here is where we have more control over this beast because you can control not only the number of e-mails, but also their effectiveness. And if you can do it, imagine what your team could accomplish. Let me give you a real life example.

A few years ago one of my clients was a Napa Valley winery. I've always said they were one of my favorite clients not just because I enjoyed their product but also because they were a young and energetic group. The company was growing and staff was being added on a regular basis. I was meeting with the director of the Marketing Department and she was talking about how everyone's productivity began suffering each time a new person was added to the department. When they recognized this, they created a sheet that included what to do and what not to do when it came to e-mails, phone calls, and meetings. Their communications etiquette sheet, if you will. And it was reviewed with every new employee in order to keep the group running at optimum speed.

Texts and IM

They're here to stay. They have their place. But try to keep your eye focused on what's going on or who you're talking to at the current moment.

Meetings

Webster's New World College Dictionary defines a meeting as a "gathering of people, especially to discuss or decide on matters."

Great. Then there's the book entitled *Death by Meetings* in which the author and well-known management consultant Patrick Lencioni devoted an entire book to the topic. You get the idea.

Back in 2005, Microsoft conducted a survey called the "Personal Productivity Challenge" and received thrity-eight thousand responses from two hundred countries. Respondents said they spent 5.6 hours per week in meetings and 69% thought they were unproductive meetings. It was their single biggest complaint.

Fast-forward about ten years and unproductive meetings are still one of the most discussed issues among employees. Poorly planned or conducted meetings, let alone the number of meetings, takes time from the employee's focus on working on priority issues.

But employees attending meetings aren't really the ones I'm concerned with. I'm concerned with those who are in charge of calling the meeting, running the meeting, and sharing specific expectations and timelines. Their actions are negatively impacting the productivity of a great number of people within an organization. If you tried to add up the time and multiply it by employee hourly rates, the amount would be staggering.

A Few Guidelines for Meetings

1. Prepare Before

One of the most important steps to making a meeting effective happens before the meeting ever takes place. It's creating a purposeful agenda. And it's frequently the one thing skipped because someone wants to "wing it."

Why is it so important? Because the agenda helps you *narrow down exactly* what you want to discuss and what you want the outcome to be, and these two things determine *who to invite*. If you can't distill what you want into a specific point, you stand a chance of having multiple topics hatch during the meeting, inevitably losing focus, getting off track, and wasting time. You need to treat your meeting the way you would set a goal—it needs to be clear, specific, and time lined. If you set an expectation that you want participants to prepare for the meeting, then they need to have the agenda in hand more than ten minutes beforehand, so I suggest sending it out at least 24-48 hours in advance. Of course, that means that you, as host, need to be organized and focused enough to do so. Your time management skills definitely come into play.

A strong agenda should include:

1. Date of meeting

2. Time of meeting

3. Time line, topic, name, and title of who's delivering it (i.e., 8:40-9:00 a.m., Business update, John Doe, VP of Operations).

Another complaint I often hear is people who leave the meeting and say they are not sure why they were invited to begin with. If you're calling the meeting, spend some time in deciding who *really* needs to be in the meeting. And if you run across people you're not sure need to be there, contact them individually by explaining the agenda and asking if they would like or need an invitation or just a report of the outcome.

2. Prepare During

Okay, so the Agenda has gone out and now it's time for you to prepare your approach for conducting the meeting—a meeting that's worth everyone's time. So here are a few ideas:

- Build a reputation for starting on time.

- Open the meeting by sharing why attendees were invited.

- Ask everyone to turn off their electronics or, at the very least, put them on vibrate. Some companies have employees park their phones outside the meeting room.

- Explain what they can expect at the end of the meeting.

- Ask participants to keep comments to two minutes. This does a couple things. It helps you finish on time, and it gets the participants to understand that they need to think provide their comments in a more focused manner rather than just rambling Also, ask participants not to repeat what's already been said but to consciously think about adding new comments.

- Take notes or ask someone to take notes on a pre-printed form that relates to agreed upon commitments and time frames. It's a simple form that includes three columns: the issue, the person responsible for it, and the date the findings will be reported back. If this form is completed during the meeting, it can be scanned and sent out as meeting notes without involving any extra work.

- Make sure the notes include decision(s) made, and if none were, what the next step actually is toward moving the decision(s) forward.

- And last but not least, develop a reputation for ending on time.

3. Prepare for the After

This one's pretty simple.

- Take your completed notes/form, scan it, and send it out to attendees with your thanks and next steps.

- Take the time to identify and name who is responsible for

following up with assigned tasks.

Maybe this will help you remember:

M ake a decision on the topic
E xtend an invitation via agenda
E nsure you begin and end on time
T ask everyone to speak for only two minutes
I nvite everyone to speak
N ever let someone monopolize
G et next steps outlined clearly
S ummarize and send notes

Okay, so these are some approaches for helping you make meetings more productive. But what about one-on-one conversations?

4. One-on-One Conversations

Meetings are about someone communicating with a group. But we all have one-on-one conversations in person or on the phone. And there are a few other things to consider with this scenario. This information will pertain to supervising someone, but I'll cover that in a later chapter on delegating.

Listening is probably 50% of communicating effectively. I'm sure you've been in a situation where you've heard two people talking "over" one another. They're talking and sharing their own individual thoughts and opinions, but not really listening to what the other person is saying.

As the saying goes, they "like to hear themselves talk," so two-way communication isn't really happening. Empathic listening is a major part of being a great communicator and of having an engaged workforce, and engaged workforces tend to have much higher productivity levels.

You also need to make sure your message is clear and set expectations about what you're needing or trying to achieve by the end of the conversation.

But there's one other thing that's really helpful and I didn't really realize the impact it had until I sat down and thought about it. It's not always *what* the person is saying but *how* the person is saying something because how they say it can impact what you hear and, more importantly, what you don't hear. And that impacts what you do and don't do.

After I realized the importance of this and its impact on productivity, I started exploring how I could learn more and find some tools that could help me with clients. And then my friend Shawn Kent Hayashi introduced me to DISC assessments. Shawn owns Your Talent at Work and she is a master at helping employees learn and grow by identifying their communications style. I have become certified in DISC and use it frequently with clients when I feel employee communication issues are impeding their productivity.

DISC is an acronym for the four the different communication styles: Dominant, Intuitive, Steady, and Compliant. It's an online assessment you take and receive a full profile on your personal dominant and sub-dominant styles. But it's also to understand all four of the styles so you can adjust your communication to the style of the person talking to you. This is frequently the same style they use or exhibit when they e-mail you. The DISC assessment is a really valuable tool in helping employees listen to what is being said without being distracted by the way it's being said through simply understanding the other person's communication style. It's a time saver, a team builder, and a great tool to use to improve job performance and productivity.

Daily Huddles

One of the approaches I feel strongly about is the daily huddle, sometimes referred to as "dailies." These are short meetings—usually under fifteen minutes—with very specific agendas.

One-on-One Huddle

I almost always recommend a one-on one huddle in these two situations:

- The employee is a new hire

- The employee has been promoted

When an employees are new hires they have lots of questions and access to their supervisor during the course of the day may be difficult or non-existent. If a daily morning huddle is in place and adhered to, it gives both the employee and the supervisor the chance to get to answer pressing questions, get to know one another, pass information along, and even define preferences in terms of how each of them works. Questions may be as fundamental as the day-to-day requirements of the job. I find this is approach particularly effective when it comes to executives and their administrative assistants. A large part of the role of administrative assistants is to help their boss remain more productive. This can't be done when there is restricted communication. They need full access and a daily huddle can help accomplish this.

When employees are promoted, they usually need some guidance on how their responsibilities have changed and what is expected. And if the employees have been promoted from within their own unit, guidance is critical because not only has their role with their supervisor changed, but their role with their peers has changed as well. This can cause some anxiety employees can manage in a couple ways.

They can choose to figure things out themselves through trial and error including an occasional meeting with their supervisor or they can continually come to their supervisor with questions throughout the day. Either approach isn't productive for the employee, the staff or the supervisor. So being proactive and setting up a daily huddle can mitigate a lot of these issues.

Team Huddle

Just as huddles are effective for two people, they are equally effective for teams. With team huddles you can begin every day with sharing news, accomplishments, concerns, asking for something that's needed, and hearing what others might need. It enables employees, team leaders, and managers to share news and helps the team more fully understand the course of the day ahead. It also helps them be more productive.

Of course, you can always try some of the approaches I've read about that are being used by some startups. In one, the owner had daily fifteen-minute team huddles where everyone stands during the meeting. This resulted in team members giving pretty concise answers in order to end the meeting sooner!

Another startup approach—one of the most unique I've ever heard—included an owner who had everyone drink a full glass of water before the meeting and the first person needing to visit the bathroom ended the meeting. Hmm.

The One Thing to Remember:

It's not just what we say but how we say it that impacts others.

Three Things You Can Do:

1. Consider having yourself and your team take a DISC assessment so you can learn how to adapt and communicate more effectively.

2. Begin to listen with more intent.

3. Set clear expectations in every discussion.

Write down *one* thing you're going to do differently or change.

The Last Word

*"If you had to identify, in one word,
the reason why the human race has not achieved
and never will achieve its full potential,
that word would be meetings."*

Dave Barry

CHAPTER 14

Productivity Pothole #2: Interruptions, distractions, and overcommitments

Every few years the types of questions I get asked about tend to be around the types of issues currently facing employees. In the early days it was the challenge of actually identifying what was most important. Years went by and the topic shifted to frustration with e-mail and how to handle the volume. But the winner these past few years has definitely been questions on how to manage interruptions and distractions.

When I first started in this business the average interruption was three per hour—one every twenty minutes or so. Then that statistic doubled. Then it doubled again. Today the information out there is that we experience twenty interruptions per hour or *one every three minutes.* And research says it takes about twenty-five minutes or so to climb back into what you were doing at the same level of intensity and concentration. So it's not just the loss of real time, it's the loss of focus.

Academics complain a great deal about how students today have technology at their fingertips for answers they need, but they do not recognize or practice the importance of critical thinking. Uninterrupted focus is needed to work on priorities, issues, problems, and challenges.

This is a very important topic in your time management and personal productivity challenges because it's about *setting boundaries*. With yourself and others. This isn't always easy, but it's a skill worth learning.

First Step

The first step is to find out where your interruptions are coming from. There is software that can track how much time you spend on the Internet, but make sure you have something more comprehensive than that. I usually suggest keeping what I call a **TimeBank**© log. It's a log you maintain for a couple weeks to record 1) where your time is being spent and 2) how long you spend on each activity.

Activity examples include: meetings, calls, e-mail, *interruptions from others*, etc. Take the total time spent in each activity and divide it by the number of hours you work in a week to get a percentage.

Employees who take the time to go through this exercise are always shocked at the results—especially when they see how much time they spend on things that don't move their priorities forward.

To a given degree, human beings have always been a major source of interruptions, but now we have technology adding a new layer to the mix. So let's take a minute and look at the anatomy of interruptions and distractions.

Interruptions

There are two types of interruptions—internal and external.

Internal interruptions are when you distract yourself. I'm not talking about taking a break. I'm talking about an intentional action to stop doing something important to do something less important. It might include things like ...

- Checking your phone every five minutes

- Checking your e-mail every five minutes

- Checking your social media every five minutes

- Responding to each and every text that comes through at the moment it arrives

- Maintaining the e-mail feature that lets you know each time a new e-mail arrives in your inbox

- Arranging your desk to sit facing a window, and the reason isn't because daydreaming helps you develop new ideas but simply a way for you to consistently imagine where you'd rather be

- Watching your phone while attending a meeting

If you're brave enough, technology can help. You can always use the software Rescuetime which shows you how much time you're spending on the Internet.

Multitasking

Since we're talking about internal interruptions I can't forget to say something about multitasking. This is one of my favorite illustrations of distracting yourself from something you need to keep your eye on and the consequences.

"A multitasking twenty-five year old was driving a flat-bed truck carrying two motorcycles and towing two trucks. He was talking on one cell phone while texting on another and accidentally crashed into a house, ending up with himself, his truck, and part of his cargo submerged under water."

In this case, no one was hurt. It could have been worse.

According to Google, it's defined as:

- The simultaneous execution of more than one program or task by a single computer processor

- The handling of more than one task at the same time by a single person

For those who grew up on technology the idea of multitasking is fairly common. This generation was multitasking before mobile while they sat at their desk. And since many have grown up knowing *only* mobile, both the ability and the temptation to do several things at once anywhere at any time is part of their technological experience—their DNA, if you will.

For those of us who did not grow up with technology, focus and doing one thing at a time is how we got things done. We finished projects by concentrating on one thing at a time until we got there. We didn't experience the number or types of interruptions we experience today.

I can see both sides, but my theory is that it has a lot to do with how you define multitasking.

For example, if I put in a load of laundry, start boiling water to make pasta, and check my e-mail all at the same time, I'm technically multitasking. So yes, I multitask. I suspect all of us do within this definition.

Here's where it breaks down. Multitasking takes a toll on the product of your work because of the disruption of focus. And we all need focus and sometimes critical thinking during that period to come up with some of our best work or at least work that is required. Work you are responsible for in the long run. When you let multitasking interfere with that type of needed focus, you diminish the result. It may not stress you—you may be used to it—but it can and frequently does negatively affect outcomes.

After all the discussion and research pointing to and proving how multitasking isn't good for you or your brain, I suspect it will continue. Because we're human beings and change is sometimes hard.

You get the idea. The first step is to begin practicing the idea of remaining focused. The second is acknowledging that internal interruptions are part of what prevents you from doing so.

So what to do?

Scheduling and adhering to specific scheduled daily breaks in the action is one way. If you have a schedule that isn't quite that predictable, another solution is to take a break when you can by making a deal with yourself. If you finish X, then you can do Y. It's called the *if-then* approach and I'll talk about it more in the chapter on procrastination. The general idea is to dangle a proverbial carrot in front of yourself by making a rule with *yourself up front* to make it easier for your brain to automatically regulate your behavior.

External Interruptions

External interruptions are things we don't anticipate and can't control. They just happen. I'm specifically talking here about other people coming to your workspace because they have a question. And during the course of the day this happens many times by either the same person or others, day in and day out. And yes, it's true that sometimes that person is your boss. So let's assume some ground rules.

Priority contacts. If a high number of interruptions come from your boss or perhaps a family member, they're more than likely already acknowledged priority contacts. But if the interruptions are frequent and continual to the point of finding it difficult to work then be proactive about your needs. Open a dialogue with your boss and ask:

- If you can have a two-to-three-minute daily huddle to see what types of questions/issues they may have on their mind.

- Let your boss know what you'll be working on that day, your priorities, and your deadlines.

- Share the concept of setting a certain block of time daily to work on priorities. This block can be the same time every day or a certain amount of time based on your schedule, but it needs to be daily.

Everyone else. In your company, there are probably varying approaches on how effectively employees are managing their own time. You probably already know who is usually on time with deadlines and who isn't, who is generally late to meetings and who isn't, etc. The obvious thing is that you may be impacted by some of these folks, but you can't control the issue. However, you can control how you respond.

First step? Determine how many interruptions you're subject to in a day, who they come from, and how long they last using a tool similar to the **TimeBank©** approach I mentioned earlier. You could also use a simple spreadsheet, audio device, or whatever else might work for you to record this information. The result is being able to identify the main culprits who may be cutting up your day, unknowingly or not.

Sometimes it's simple enough to not require a log, as I learned years ago.

At the time I was working for a company as the operations director and interfaced with sales and engineering. Dick was our project manager and he started coming to my office on a daily basis and "visiting." The visits were friendly enough, but they didn't really seem to have a point. After a while I realized Dick was stopping by to chat not because of any significant work-related issues, but because he wanted a treat from a bowl of candy I had begun keeping in my office. By having this bowl of goodies, I actually *trained* Dick to stop by and interrupt me! Needless to say, I got rid of the bowl and the candies.

Dick and I still had social conversation, but it was generally at lunchtime.

You get the idea. Identify where your time goes and to whom so you can more clearly identify what you can do to reclaim your time.

I believe it was Verne Harnish in *Mastering The Rockefeller Habits* who said something like when someone stops by your door and asks if you've got a minute, it's never a minute. If it's an emergency or crisis, it's sensitive and you pay attention, depending on whose emergency or crisis we're talking about.

But if repeat interruptions stem from peers or team members who have a habit of interrupting, it's important to develop an approach for handling these situations. When someone interrupts you and you choose to participate in a discussion rather than set a boundary, you're actively climbing out of your priorities and agenda and into theirs. *Managing interruptions and distractions is about setting boundaries—with yourself and others.*

In her book *Power Phrases*, Meryl Runion talks about ways and gives examples of how to say no. In my workshops I have a section I label "learning to say no *gracefully*." I developed this type of approach after reading an interview years ago with the author Alice Schroeder who was assigned to write Warren Buffet's biography entitled *The Snowball*.

She was asked what she learned from Warren Buffet. Most readers and audiences probably suspected the answer to be something along the lines of a financial mantra. I'm paraphrasing here, but as I remember, Ms. Schroeder responded that she had already had a career as a successful analyst and wasn't really looking for that type of information for herself. The one thing she said that impressed her more than anything was Warren Buffet's ability to say no.

I'm sure you can imagine the demands on the time of someone like Warren Buffet. But then I hear people say that he has all kinds of help and doesn't own a computer. Yes, he has three executive assistants that take care of distinct and separate issues for him. No, he doesn't have a computer. But he does clearly recognize the importance of goals, priorities, and the value of his time. That's why his approach looks something like this:

- He identifies his goals at the first of every year.

- Then he determines where he'll spend his time—his priorities based on his goals.

- He communicates this information to his team.

- And for those who contact him looking for time or expertise but are not part of his identified priority list, his staff is trained and instructed to provide these individuals with names and resources of others who may be able to help them.

He is effectively setting boundaries by gracefully saying *no* and offering alternatives.

And you can do the same.

It's about finding a way to respond to someone in an approach I call it "Let's Make a Deal."

Let's Make A Deal

Here are two steps you can take to help you begin successfully setting boundaries with others once they've told you what their question is about:

Step 1: Share your why. Tell people you can't help them right now and tell them why. Hopefully it's because you're focused on a priority and would like to continue working on it. Telling people why usually helps them to understand your side of the situation.

Step 2: Make a deal. Then add, "But let's make a deal to meet around

11:30 a.m. (or another time) and we can talk about it then when you've got my full attention."

This does two things for your visitors: It sends the message you're setting some boundaries around your own priorities and it lets them know their question is important enough to deserve your full attention so you're offering an alternative meeting time. You're not slamming the door on them. You're not screaming no. You're not throwing them out. You're saying no gracefully. IF you do this at the appropriate time with the appropriate person, it can be very effective—it just takes practice.

Of course, sometimes you don't get the response you want because others have their own time frames and time management challenges or they're late, worried, etc. When this happens, they keep pushing for you to meet with them at that moment.

Let me give you a real life example of how someone handled this in a grocery store.

I was in the checkout line at a grocery store and there was a woman in front of me with a child who was about seven or eight years old. He kept asking if he could have the candy he was eyeing as they were standing in line. The mom said "not right now." The child continued. The mom said "maybe later." The child continued. Then she said, "Keep this up and you won't get any." After a while, the child continued. It wasn't until she stopped and said, "It's right before suppertime and I don't want you spoiling your appetite by eating candy. I'll buy the candy for you now but it will go in the bag and you won't be able to have it until you've finished your dinner." The child stopped asking because she gave him the *no for now* and made a deal. He got what he wanted and so did she. I think moms are pretty effective at this "make a deal" thing, so we all probably have something to learn from them!

All in all, we can't stop interruptions, and there are certain ones we wouldn't really want to stop. Whether it's internal or external causes, we can only move toward managing ourselves to manage the situation by setting some boundaries.

So determine where your interruptions and distractions are coming from and then use the approach I've outlined—or one of your own—to deflect them. As your GPS would say, "Reroute your course."

A Word About Mindfulness

There has been a growing movement for learning to be more mindful during our workday. It's similar to meditation in that mindfulness asks you to become and remain in the here and now. There's nothing you can do about yesterday and little you can do about tomorrow except preoccupy yourself with worry. Therefore, remaining focused in the present is less stressful, improves your mood, and frequently results in better productivity. If you're not interested in meditating then at least try to at least practice mindfulness.

If you're feeling overloaded the next best thing to do is to change tasks and let your mind wander. Letting your mind wander is healthy. It helps with creativity and innovation, minimizes brain and energy drain, and can change your spirit and perspective.

Harvey Schechter wrote an article in *The Globe and Mail* titled "Brainy Tips to Boost " Productivity." In the post he suggested three tips:

1. Let your mind wander because a lot of important stuff happens while we do that.

2. Exercise improves your concentration immediately and can help you feel more relaxed.

3. Clutter is not a good distraction. Get your workspace to work for you and provide a clear work environment.

The One Thing to Remember:

Managing interruptions is about setting boundaries
for yourself and others.

Three Things You Can Do:

1. Use the TimeBank© for a week or two to identify your detractors and determine what lost time is costing you.

2. Practice the three-step approach: acknowledge, say no gracefully, let's make a deal.

3. Keep at it—it takes time.

Write down *one* thing you're going to do differently or change.

The Last Word

*"The difference between successful people
and really successful people
is that really successful people
say 'no' to everything."*

Warren Buffet

CHAPTER 15

Productivity Pothole #3: Delayed decisions

Let's start out strong here.

Procrastination is a deal breaker. No reason to step around it.

It's the one behavior that not only stops you from doing what you need and want to be doing, but also adds a load of frustration, anxiety, stress to yourself, and frequently to others.

I'm not talking about the type of procrastination that happens every so often when faced with something you don't want to do. We're human and we all procrastinate about something at some point in life. I'm talking about when procrastination has become a consistent negative effect on your life. Something that others identify as *you*.

In fact, one of the most frequent complaints I've heard about today's workforce, from supervisors and staff alike, is about employees not doing what they committed to do. It can mean not producing something to begin with, not following through on a commitment, or putting it off until the last minute. This type of behavior results in chaos, havoc, frustration, poor customer service, poor productivity, general bad feelings among coworkers, and poor performance reviews.

Where do you begin?

First of all, recognize that procrastination is a habit that started when you were younger and stayed with you right into your adult years.

When I get calls from parents who have had children go off to college I usually know what the call is about. It generally seems their college kids are struggling with becoming and remaining organized, getting to class on time, getting homework completed, etc. When they lived at home, they frequently had parents helping them either by doing something the children consistently put off or reminding them to do something which was promptly tuned out. Now these young adults are on their own and no one is there to catch them, and it can result in poor grades or even dismissal.

Secondly, procrastination can be seen as something else. Perfectionism is a type of procrastination, but many of us think of it as simply a behavior needing to be perfect or have things perfectly done. So it stands to reason that in order to be able to work on your procrastination tendencies, you need to be able to identify your style. And to do this, you might need the help of a psychologist. That's why I love the book *It's About Time* by Dr. Linda Sapadin.

Dr. Sapadin is a psychologist and she wrote this book back in 1996. Today you can find her on LinkedIn and various other places on the Internet. I've never found a book that provided as much information on ways to conquer procrastination as this one. It has an assessment to help you identify your dominant and sub-dominant style of procrastination. Here are the six styles she identifies:

> Perfectionist
> Dreamer
> Worrier
> Defier
> Crisis Maker
> Overdoer

When I took the assessment I discovered I was a perfectionist-worrier. Here's how that impacted my business when I first began.

At the time Dr. Sapadin's book was published my business was relatively new and it was the first time I'd ventured out into being an entrepreneur. Much of this newfound profession included lots of marketing. I wasn't even sure what marketing was about, so I really didn't address it in my very informal and unsophisticated business plan. But I quickly found out it wasn't something that could be ignored and decided part of my marketing would include writing articles. And so I began.

I would write the article, read it again the next day, and revise it. I would revise it again the next day, and the next, and the one after that. The article was never good enough for me. I was never satisfied. It wasn't *perfect*.

I kept writing articles and this same approach continued over the next three to four months. More articles but still no publication. What if people didn't read the article? What if there was a typo I didn't catch? Prospects may not hire me. I was *worrying* my way to not doing anything! Mine is a great profile of a perfectionist-worrier procrastinator. All this anxiety built up and absolutely nothing got done.

Then one day I woke up.

There was a woman in one of the professional groups I belonged to at the time who began her business about the same time I began mine. She was struggling with some of the same issues but there was one main difference: She got her marketing materials out there while mine were still sitting in my desk drawer. Were they perfect? By her own admission, no they weren't. Was she worried? Sometimes, but she never thought it would cost her business. She just assumed it was part of the process.

And that threw my "ah-ha" light on. There was no point in worrying, because that didn't really accomplish anything for me or my business. And there was no point in thinking it had to be perfect because few things are perfect. They're simply the best they can be at that moment. I needed to think differently. So I began publishing my articles. Did one get published that had a typo? Yes. Did it cost me my business? No. Live and learn.

Over the years I developed an approach for myself that has evidently been researched and given a name. It's the *if-then* approach.

If This Then That

Peter Gollwitzer is the psychologist who first studied *if-then* planning. It basically says the brain can send itself an automatic message to begin to do whatever the message was about without all the to-do lists, bells and whistles, and assorted reminders. The *if-then* statement contains a specific trigger that gets you to do something automatically, similar to a habit. It embeds in your brain and sounds like this:

- If it's Friday, then I'll complete my expense report.

- If it's a weekday, then I'll go to the gym as soon as I wake up.

Back to my marketing-perfectionist-worrier-procrastination dilemma. Once I realized what I was doing, I knew I had to consider some type of *self-imposed rule*. So this was the deal I made with myself.

If I put my article in the drawer for three days, **then** on the third day I make a final revision and publish it the same day.

It was very specific—no wiggle room and it drove me to a next action that was already determined. I didn't have to think about it and the minute I put an article in the drawer, my brain knew about the deal I made with myself. I still practice it to this day, more than twenty years later.

When I sat down to write this book the publisher obviously gave me a deadline. So I went to my calendar and set up appointments with myself in order to keep me focused and moving forward.
As excited as I was about this project, putting it on my calendar didn't

seem to be working. Other things cropped up that were more important, yet the deadline date remained fixed. And I knew myself well enough to know that the hardest part for me wasn't what I was going to say—it was getting started. As Mark Twain said, "The secret of getting ahead is getting started." So I started worrying.

Uh oh. The idea that I was procrastinating again around writing reared its ugly head. So I created an *if-then* scenario for myself.

If I have the time slotted in my calendar, **then** I'll write the first sentence of a chapter.

And this is exactly what happened. My *if-then* approach helped make my actions automatic and without much more than normal stress because it was a trigger. Once I wrote the first sentence, my writing continued for three and a half to four hours every time. I finished the first draft of the book in record time.

If-then scenarios are frequently used to in relation to goal setting for individuals or teams. However, the application is far-reaching for many types of situations, and I think a very helpful tool for overcoming procrastination tendencies, regardless of your style.

Stop now and create a specific *if-then* scenario for something you have been struggling with, personal or professional. See what happens.

If you work with or supervise someone who is a procrastinator and their habits are causing problems for themselves and coworkers or other staff members, take the time to explain this approach and help them set up a couple *if-then* scenarios. You can find out more about the research and approach on the Internet and by looking at the work of Dr. Heidi Grant Halvorson.

As always, practice around these types of habits or behaviors takes an investment in understanding, dedication, and time but is well worth it for the peace of mind and improved personal productivity waiting for you to experience.

The One Thing to Remember:

Procrastination is a habit that can be changed.

Three Things You Can Do:

1. Identify your style of procrastination.

2. Redirect and reframe your thoughts.

3. Try out the *if-then* approach.

Write down *one* thing you're going to do differently or change.

The Last Word

*"The best time to plant a tree is twenty years ago.
The second best time is today."*

Chinese Proverb

CHAPTER 16

Productivity Pothole #4: <u>**Delegating ≠ micromanaging**</u>

How is delegating tied to your productivity?

Simply put, it's the one thing that leverages your time to work on more important tasks which are generally things that only you can or should be doing.

Learning to delegate can move *you* into ...

- Managing rather than doing

- Focusing on higher priority issues

- Focusing on more strategic issues

- Putting decision making at the appropriate level

- Improving trust between yourself and your direct reports

- Identifying employees for new assignments or promotion

Look what it does for the *employee* as well:

- Provides them with new opportunities and experiences

- Builds initiative, skills, knowledge, and creativity

- Improves confidence which in turn builds self-esteem

- Helps them see and appreciate their role in the organization as a whole

And consider what it does for the *organization*:

- Reduces conflict because communication and feedback increase

- Improves loyalty and team cohesiveness which helps improve morale

- Increases individual skills in planning and organization

- Helps identify talent for selection of future leaders

- Can produce more value-added results

Just by reading this list you realize if done properly, delegating tasks or projects is a win/win all the way around. However, through the years I've noticed that many supervisors have never really had in-depth training on how to delegate *effectively*.

I realize training has been either reduced or moved to online venues by the economic challenges of the past few years, so many supervising employees have had to dig out their own information on learning this skill. The result is that over time, I've seen an increase in micromanaging and the resulting stress.

Take Carmen for example.

She was an individual in a department who eventually became a team lead. No problem. She did such a great job that she was eventually promoted and supervised eight staff and an administrative assistant.

The problem was she wasn't prepared for this role and ended up micromanaging and doing everyone else's work. She struggled, her direct reports struggled, and trust, morale, and productivity were at an all-time low. She wasn't prepared because she...

- Wasn't sure exactly what was expected of her

- Had no training or understanding of what supervision involved

- Was thrown into the task without much direction or preparation

- Experienced no routine, ongoing communication with her supervisor

- Found her supervisor was either not available or accessible regarding the type of expertise she needed

- What she did well was never acknowledged

What to do? Here are some basic ideas on how to become a supervisor or manager who delegates effectively. If you follow the guidelines and steps I outline below, you'll save time by experiencing fewer interruptions where the employee needs to ask questions, stand a better chance that the project is completed correctly, thoroughly, and on time, grow an employee, and identify a leader. And you'll have more time to work on the important things on your plate.

What to Delegate

Sometimes a supervisor doesn't know exactly what to delegate. What items? Too much? Too little? Here are some things that can and probably should be delegated to the right employee at the right time:

- Repetitive tasks

- Information gathering

- Attending meetings for gathering information, when appropriate

- Tasks or projects in which the supervisor may be overqualified

- Tasks or projects the supervisor might not want to do for a variety of reasons

- Some things the supervisor may actually do well but doesn't have the time due to other priority issues

What NOT to Delegate

Some things shouldn't be delegated. Feel free to add or subtract items based on your company's policies.

- Politically sensitive material

- Bad news

- Confidential matters

- Strategic matters

- Difficult customer negotiations

- Disciplinary matters

- Issues involving other employee's performance

- Items requiring a technical skill set the employee may not have

- Something your supervisor asked you to personally handle

Authority, Responsibility, Accountability

Many years ago, when I first started supervising, my boss took the time to explain the difference between authority, responsibility, and accountability, and it's worth repeating:

Authority is the right to act and make decisions. Be clear with the employees on how much authority they have when it comes to this project. Setting boundaries is an important part of this.

Responsibility is an obligation to perform a job assignment. It is the employee's responsibility to complete the assignment and seek whatever tools are necessary to do so.

Accountability involves answering questions re: actions and decisions. This is true of every employee in the organization, not just the employee assigned a project.

Items to Consider When Giving the Assignment

- **History.** Most employees like to understand how their assignment came about, so a brief history is helpful.

- **Context.** Another question an employee might have, but did not ask, is how this project fits into the organization's bigger strategic picture. Context helps employees see a fuller picture of why their work is important.

- **Future importance**. You can and should continue by sharing the importance of what they will be doing for the future of their role, the team, and the organization.

Initial Meeting

When entering the speaking profession, there is a saying that most speakers traditionally hear right off the bat. There are three things you always tell an audience:

1. Tell them what you're going to tell them.

2. Tell them.

3. Tell them what you told them.

Something similar to this takes place when you finally sit down with the employee to give them an assignment. These suggestions may or may not seem obvious, but they're worth covering as a reminder if nothing else.

- **Ask employees to bring their calendar.** At the end of the meeting you'll want to set up recurring short huddles/ meetings to hear how they're doing and see if they have questions or need additional resources. This can be weekly, every other week, or monthly. Whatever works.

- **Suggest at employees be prepared to take notes.** A lot of ground will be covered and you'll want to make sure they capture what's needed.

- **Let employees know up front that at the end of your meeting you'll be asking them to review what they heard.** Let them know that this is so *you* can be confident *you* covered everything. It tends to keep an employee alert and listening.

- **Encourage employees to ask questions.** Sometimes employees don't want to appear unknowing so they only take information in without asking for clarification. Tell them you'll be somewhat concerned if they don't have any questions because this may be a new skill set for them and you want to make sure they're prepared the best they can be.

- **Be specific.** Explain what you need to explain about the project making sure you are specific with deadline dates, resources, and potential pitfalls. And again, explain the impact of their work. Think it through and put it on paper because it's easy to forget all the details and you don't want to waste precious time—yours or theirs.

- **Conclude the meeting with a review.** It can sound something like this:

  I just want to make sure you have everything you need and that the project work begins without a hitch, so I'd really appreciate if you could review what we covered today.

  Or

  Before you get started, I just want to make sure we're on the same page. Please tell me your understanding of this assignment.

Then make sure you have dates for your next meeting and future meetings.

Review Meetings

However frequently or infrequently you have review sessions, make them as important as a meeting with your own boss. Try not to cancel.

If the employee is on target with their assignment and you're pleased with the progress, these meetings can be easy and result in significantly improved performance. But normally what you find is there are some areas where the employee may be struggling or at the very least needing a bit of help, so the meeting is your chance to help that person develop.

Here are some general guidelines to help the employee be successful:

- **Additional direction**. If employees are off base, struggling, or not clear about the project, it's probably because they need some additional direction. In this case, provide specific direction and ask employees to tell you what they heard you say.

- **Action and reaction**. Ask for the employees' input on certain items. They may be uncertain about a decided approach and need you to pose questions by asking about challenges. If their challenge involves another person, the employee may need to role-play the approach in order for them to feel confident about their communication with others. Also, don't forget to ask for possible solutions to challenges employees have identified so they may share their thoughts.

- **Preparation.** Employees may have time management challenges potentially affecting the deadline date. Encourage them to block or set time aside every day or week to work on the project. Tell them to gather all the information they'll need ahead of time to be ready to dive in when these blocks of time come up.

- **Specific actions and behaviors.** Depending on the situation, you may find need to coach the employee for specific actions or behaviors needed to bring the project to a successful completion.

- **Concrete suggestions.** Reviews where employees are off course should be anything but vague. For their growth, they need specific and concrete suggestions they can implement in order to be successful.

- **Smaller bites.** Sometimes employees get into a project and become overwhelmed. This can even happen in your initial meeting. The best approach to any large project is to break it into smaller pieces with different timelines. Offering smaller bites over time can help build a rhythm and some confidence, as well as keep the employee from becoming overwhelmed.

- **Encouragement.** We all need a sense of belonging, accomplishment, and confidence. Do what you can, when appropriate or needed, to bolster the employee's newfound role.

Giving Direction

The types of direction you give can depend on the project and the experience of the individual involved. The supervisor's level of instruction can be stated in many ways:

- Ask the team for *input on the project*

- Ask the team to "let me know *what happens*"

- "Let me know what *action you took*"

- "I'd like your *recommendations on the solution*"

- "Just *let me know*"

Acknowledgment and Reward

So let's say the employee has successfully finished the project. How do you acknowledge this? What do you do? You can:

- Acknowledge the employee publicly

- Reward accordingly

- Add some responsibilities on a permanent basis

- Add more responsibilities and projects as they can be handled

But there's one last thing I think is important. In the book *1001 Ways to Reward Employees*, the authors have surveyed companies for several years asking employees what for them would be the ultimate reward for a job well done and then ranking their top five answers. Bosses frequently say they think the employee will say money is the most important. That being said, employees have never mentioned money in the top five. Can you guess what employee responses were for the top five rewards?

#5. The manager holds a *morale-building meeting* to celebrate the success.

#4. The manager *publicly recognizes* the employee.

#3. The organization *uses performance* as a basis for promotion.

#2. The manager *writes a note* to the employee about their performance.

And the top answer?

#1. The manager *goes to the employee's office* and *personally congratulates* them.

Just imagine how you would react if your boss practiced the number one answer above. I would think that the return on investment practicing this approach would be well worth it.

Delegating to a Remote or Virtual Assistant

When you're using the services of a virtual assistant or if your assistant is working remotely, you would follow the same *general* steps I've outlined in this chapter, omitting the obvious ones that would pertain only in situations where you are supervising an employee. The idea is to set expectations and desired outcomes.

I hope this information prepares you, expands your thinking, or was a useful review of how delegating can build your workforce and leverage your time.

The One Thing to Remember:

> Delegating not only leverages your time—
> it also develops your employees.

Three Things You Can Do:

1. Decide what you will delegate and to whom.

2. Make regular follow-up meetings a priority.

3. Be organized so you can be ready to use the time you gain to focus on your own priorities.

Write down *one* thing you're going to do differently or change.

The Last Word

"When you were made a leader you weren't given a crown,
you were given the responsibility
to bring out the best in others."

Jack Welch

CHAPTER 17

Getting it all done

There's lots of information in this book. It's an accumulation of over forty years in business and what I've learned along the way. But the work is ahead of you and can be daunting ... so how do you get started?

Set a goal. What do you want to accomplish, change, or do? Pick one thing you can do to improve your productivity and ask yourself if you're connected to it. Do you own it? Does it motivate you? If not, keep looking.

Prioritize. What's the most important thing you have to do to get started? Break down your actions into smaller steps and tackle them one at a time. Taking this approach helps you feel like you're taking a stroll instead of climbing a mountain. Begin today with a small project and keep moving forward from there.

Become focused and set boundaries. We usually underestimate the number of things that compete for our attention. Identify what those things are and learn to set boundaries so you can continue to do the best work possible in the role you play.

Be patient and realistic. We also tend to underestimate the amount of work it will take to make change. Don't waste time and energy by setting unrealistic expectations. It's time and energy you could be using elsewhere to do something productive ... or fun! Maybe an accountability partner can help you achieve your goal. Identify someone and ask that person to:

- Support you in your goal
- Encourage you when you find you've gotten off track
- Think about becoming an accountability partner
- Celebrate your successes

And don't discount the concept of creating a group of other individuals whose goal is the same or similar to yours. You can share resources, tips, recognition, and support and review best practices. There is power in numbers!

Be flexible.

Not everything in this book will work for you. Evaluate what works and what doesn't and make reasonable adjustments.

I know you can do it. You need to believe you can do it. You're armed with more information than you had before and it's time to apply it. Because, as my friend Dan Stalp says, "Education without execution is entertainment."

So go ahead, take the first small step toward making your life and work less stressful and more satisfying. Get organized. Get focused. Get moving!

The Last Word

*"The goal is not to be perfect by the end.
The goal is to be better today."*

Simon Sinek

CHAPTER 18

Resources

Books

I remember when there used to be one shelf of self-help books on organizing and not much more on time management or personal productivity. Now there are thousands. My favorite ones tend to be classics because other than the tools we use, little has changed when it comes to the principles of sound time management:

Getting Organized

- *Organizing from the Inside Out* by Julie Morgenstern. Great ideas for offices or homes.

- *The Organized Mind* by Dr. Daniel Levitin. Some fascinating research.

- *The Creative Habit* by Twyla Tharp. Great examples for creatives.

Performance

- *7 Habits of Highly Effective People* by Dr. Stephen Covey. A classic.

- *9 Things Successful People Do Differently* by Dr. Heidi Grant Halvorson.
  Includes additional information on If-Then approach outlined in Procrastination chapter.

- *Harvard Business Review* article by Dr. Edward Hallowell – "Overloaded Circuits: Why Smart People Underperform."

Priorities

- *The One Thing* by Gary Keller.
  This is by far the best read on prioritizing and focusing.

- *Crazy Busy* by Dr. Edward Hallowell—the man who co-authored *Driven to Distraction*.
  About the importance of remembering what's important.

Communications

- *Conversations for Change* by Shawn Kent Hayashi.
  An assessment approach to improving communications.

Setting Boundaries

- *Power Phrases* by Meryl Runion.
  Learning more about how to set boundaries by saying *no*.

Procrastination

- *It's About Time* by Dr. Linda Sapadin.
  Six styles of procrastination plus assessment.

Making Change

- *Change Anything* by Kerry Patterson.
  A well-researched and interesting approach to making change.

Software and Apps

There are over one million apps out there to help. They're a big part of the tools that help us be more productive. Here are some that I've used, tried out, or heard about that you may also find helpful:

To-Do Lists

- **Todoist** – For Gmail

- **Any.do** – Syncs across all devices

- **Rememberthemilk** – For remembering tasks

- **Freemind** – For mind mapping rather than list making

Shortcuts for Organizing Information/Social Media

- **Buffer**

- **Hootsuite**

- **Outofmilk** – Lists you can share. Syncs across all platforms.

- **Slidebatch** – Organizes brand content - love it

- **Zite**

- **PostItplus app** – For those of you who MUST have your Post-its!

- **Drippler** – How-to's for different phone features

Files/File Sharing

- **Evernote** – My library of many things!

- **Hopto** – iPad app helps create, edit, and manage mobile files

- **FileThis** – Automatically collects, files, tags, and organizes your online documents in a digital filing cabinet. For *personal* use/files.

- **Camcard** – To get information from your business card to your phone

- **Dropbox** – For storage and sharing files

E-mail

- **Sanebox** – Tag e-mails to come back to you in the future, delete in bulk, etc.

- **Follow Up Then** – Similar to Sanebox

- **Boomerang** (for Gmail only) – Sends e-mail at a designated future date/time

- **Unroll** – Unsubscribe from newsletters in bulk with one click

- **TextExpander** – Customized keyboard shortcuts to expand and replace text as you type!

- **Five.sentenc.es** – Unique idea on limiting # of sentences in an e-mail

- **InBoxpause** – Temporarily pauses Gmail and Google apps inbox. Chrome extension.

Meetings

- **Assistant.to** – Book meetings with one e-mail, no back and forth (!) Free for Gmail; Outlook development in progress

- **Xa.io** – *Completely* automates appointment-making tasks

- **TimeCenter** – Makes it easier for clients to make appointments

- **Clara Labs** – Artificial intelligence makes your appointments. In beta but shows promise.

Time

- **Rescuetime** – Time tracking software works in the background plus weekly reports on how you're spending your time

- **Toggl** – For time tracking

- **Ding.io** – Time tracking for freelancers and small teams

- **Limitless** – A productivity app for Chrome users

- **Stayfocusedapp.me** – Time tracker to help you stay focused

Habits

- **Procasterapp** – For iPhone. Breaks big projects into smaller manageable steps with reminders

- **Irunūrun** – Tagline: Actions speak louder than goals.

- **Winstreak**– A Strategic Coach® app to help measure your progress against your goals

- **HighExistence.com** – Thirty challenges for thirty days

- **DevelopGoodHabits.com** – Thirty-day habit challenge

- **Coach.me** (formerly LIFT) – Goal setting and tracking

Teams

- **Priority Matrix** – Managing priorities with a team

- **Asana** – For easy project management—free for teams up to fifteen people

- **Trello** – To organize projects of any kind

Odds and Ends

- **Oovoo** – Works better for me than Skype

- **Join.me** – For screen sharing

- **Redlaser** – Scans barcodes on products and compares to other locations

- **MeetMeHalfway** – Determines half way point for a meeting

- **Waze** – Live updates to reroute you due to construction, weather, etc.

- **CubeFree** – Work outside your cube and connect with others

- **TSA approval** – Not an app, but worth the $85 application fee for anyone who doesn't like taking off his or her shoes, belt, etc. You can get TSA PreCheck free through several airlines (except Southwest, who at the time of this writing only gives it to their premium travelers).

Productivity Partners Inc.

Productivity Partners, Inc. specializes in helping employees overcome time management and organizing challenges by ...

Improving performance
Increasing productivity
Reducing stress levels

In order to ...
Improve focus
Increase sales
Increase profitability
Gain some peace of mind

Provided through...
Workshops
Webinars
Assessments and coaching
Consulting
Presentations
Products

ABOUT THE AUTHOR

Cynthia Kyriazis founded her business in 1992 after twenty-five years' experience in multi-unit operations management. She is an organizing and time management coach, consultant, trainer, speaker, and author. Cynthia is past Secretary of the National Association of Professional Organizers (NAPO), Founder of NAPO-Philadelphia chapter, 2008 President of the International Society for Performance Improvement-Kansas City chapter (KC-ISPI), a national speaker and consultant to the American Coaching Association.

She has appeared on Forbes.com, WSJ.com, in the *Philadelphia Inquirer*, and the *Legal Intelligencer*, and the book *Time Management 2.0* identified her as "one of the 28 best time and productivity experts online."

For Additional Information and FREE Resources

cynthia@ProPartnersInc.com
913.649.0878
ProPartnersInc.com
Blog: MoveYourMindset.wordpress.com

Connect with Cynthia on:
LinkedIn: www.linkedin.com/in/propartnersinc
Twitter: #ProductiveYou

And Here Really Is the Last Word ...

"What we pay attention to, and how we pay attention, determines the content and quality of life."

Michael Csikszentmihalyi

Credits

This book is a work of art produced by Incorgnito Publishing Press.

Taylor Basillio
Managing Editor

Star Foos
Artist/Designer

Daria Lacy
Production Designer

Janice Bini
Chief Reader

Michael Conant
Publisher

L. Cindy Carra
Marketing Consultant

Marci Designs
Social Media/Web Consultants

February 2016
Incorgnito Publishing Press

CPSIA information can be obtained at www.ICGtesting.com
Printed in the USA
LVOW10s2132220316

480331LV00012B/213/P